ASH KEYS

ASH KEYS

New Selected Poems

Michael Longley

Foreword by
Paul Muldoon

CAPE POETRY

3 5 7 9 10 8 6 4

Jonathan Cape is part of the Penguin Random House group of companies
whose addresses can be found at global.penguinrandomhouse.com

Copyright © Michael Longley 2024
Foreword copyright © Paul Muldoon 2024

Michael Longley has asserted his right to be identified as the author of
this Work in accordance with the Copyright, Designs and Patents Act 1988

First published in the United Kingdom by Jonathan Cape in 2024

penguin.co.uk/vintage

A CIP catalogue record for this book is available from the British Library

ISBN 9781787334847

Typeset in 11/13pt Bembo Book MT Pro by Jouve (UK), Milton Keynes
Printed and bound in Great Britain by Clays Ltd, Elcograf S.p.A.

The authorised representative in the EEA is Penguin Random House Ireland,
Morrison Chambers, 32 Nassau Street, Dublin D02 YH68

Penguin Random House is committed to a sustainable future
for our business, our readers and our planet. This book is made
from Forest Stewardship Council® certified paper.

for Robin Robertson

CONTENTS

III

from **Man Lying on a Wall** (1976)

IV

from **The Echo Gate** (1979)

V

VI

VII

from **The Ghost Orchid** (1995)

VIII

from **The Weather in Japan** (2000)

IX

X

XI

XII

XIII

from **The Candlelight Master** (2020)

XIV

from **The Slain Birds** (2022)

FOREWORD

Like all major poets, Michael Longley is at once defined by his moment and, in turn, becomes a definer of it. His very first poems, some of them written while he was still an undergraduate at Trinity College, Dublin, are remarkable for the extent to which they show not only what he had learned from the great stanza-makers of the twentieth century – Larkin, Wilbur and, of course, Yeats – but also the extent to which Longley was already ploughing his own furrow:

> Lest I with fears and hopes capsize,
> By your own lights
> Sail, Body, cargoless towards surprise.
> And come, Mind, raise your sights –
> Believe my eyes.

The couplet, that mainstay of verse in English from Chaucer to Chance the Rapper, was used by Longley to considerable effect in an early poem entitled 'Persephone':

> Straitjacketed by cold and numskulled
> Now sleep the welladjusted and the skilled –
>
> The bat folds its wing like a winter leaf,
> The squirrel in its hollow holds aloof.

These four lines might be said to be quintessentially Longleyesque. First of all, there's the classical allusion to Persephone, the queen of the underworld. Throughout his career, Longley has had an uncanny ability to allow myths that might have seemed less than pertinent to be tellingly on point, particularly in his many repurposings of Homer:

> 'I get down on my knees and do what must be done
> And kiss Achilles' hand, the killer of my son.'

This final couplet from 'Ceasefire' has a Shakespearian ba-boom; those slant-rhyming couplets from 'Persephone' hint at another significant forbear – Wilfred Owen – and suggest an intriguing combination of diffidence and defiance in the face of violent action, be it poems about his father's experience in the Great War or 'Wounds', in which the Great War ghosts the murder of a bus-conductor in Northern Ireland:

> He collapsed beside his carpet-slippers
> Without a murmur, shot through the head
> By a shivering boy who wandered in
> Before they could turn the television down
> Or tidy away the supper dishes.

Though this form of 'domestic' violence may be a perversion of his fascination with 'the great indoors', it nonetheless reminds us of Longley's abiding interest in 'house and home'. We glimpse this even here in the nesting instinct of the bat 'folding its wing' and 'the squirrel in its hollow'.

The confinement of bat and squirrel suggests yet another of Longley's main impulses – towards the compact and the concise. Longley is primarily a lyric poet in that he excels in what the Academy of American Poets defines as the 'short poem, often with songlike qualities, that expresses the speaker's personal emotions and feelings'. Longley is set fairly and squarely in the tradition of the lyric poem in English, a line that runs without a snag from Richard Lovelace through Philip Larkin to himself.

The fact that a poem is compact doesn't mean it can't be compendious, and Longley has developed two main strategies in this regard. The first reflects one of our basic impulses, that of list-making. We see the beginnings of a list in the bat and the squirrel; over the years it will become a veritable carnival of animals including badgers, hares, more bats, otters, pine martens, stoats, tortoises, minnows, dolphins, kingfishers, grebes, swans, larks, ospreys, oyster-catchers, plovers, sanderlings, sedge-warblers, stonechats, snipe, snowy owls, bitterns, herons, more larks, more badgers, more hares, bees, dragonflies, moths and butterflies. For Longley, to litanise the names of animals, or flowers, or teas, or the contents of a murdered greengrocer's shop, is in essence a spiritual experience and a form of prayer.

The other, related, strategy that Longley has developed is one he borrows from Wallace Stevens and his concept of 'the whole of harmonium', whereby the many seemingly discrete individual lyrics fuse into a single 'grand poem' in which, as Stevens describes it, 'one poem proves another and the whole'.

One of the joys of this *New Selected Poems* is that readers new and old may savour the cumulative effect of Michael Longley's seemingly smallish range of obsessions. We watch an urban poet become a rural poet, equally at home in Belmullet, County Mayo, as his native Belfast. We watch a master of traditional forms turn more and more to free verse. We watch a private poet become a public poet, forced to grasp the nettle and take into account the sniper no less than the snipe:

> The nature poet turned into a war poet as if
> He could cure death with the rub of a dock leaf.

On a personal note, this volume brings back a series of powerful memories. My first encounter with Michael Longley in April 1968, after a reading in Armagh County Museum during which I heard him read 'Persephone'. A meeting of the Belfast Group at which 'Caravan' was circulated on cyclostyled sheets. The days we spent as 'minor bureaucrats' in the Arts Council and the BBC. A night in the BBC Club in Belfast on which we met the cameraman who had just returned from the scene of the Kingsmill massacre and now gave us a graphic account of its aftermath, a gruesome catalogue soon to be incorporated into 'The Linen Workers'. The untold other nights spent 'mapping the camp in wine upon the table top'. A trip we took to visit Hedli MacNeice in Kinsale to pick up several boxes of the papers of Louis MacNeice, a poet whose memory Longley has done so much to keep alive. Our fording a tidal river to get to that remote cottage in Carrigskeewaun where Longley restaked MacNeice's earlier claim on the west of Ireland. An outing to *Ain't Misbehavin'*, the musical based on

Longley's beloved Fats Waller. An afternoon spent filming him outside the ancestral house in London in which 'Second Sight' is set.

Much as I cherish these very specific reminiscences, I am also more than delighted to fall in with the generality of readers of a volume that, like the briefcase in 'Man Lying on a Wall', has 'everybody's initials on it'.

Paul Muldoon

Far from the perimeter
Of watercress and berries,
In the middle of the field
I stand talking to myself,

While the ash keys scatter
And the gates creak open
And the barbed wire rusts
To hay-ropes strung with thorns.

EPITHALAMION

These are the small hours when
Moths by their fatal appetite
That brings them tapping to get in,
 Are steered along the night
To where our window catches light.

 Who hazard all to be
Where we, the only two it seems,
Inhabit so delightfully
 A room it bursts its seams
And spills on to the lawn in beams,

 Such visitors as these
Reflect with eyes like frantic stars
This garden's brightest properties,
 Cruising its corridors
Of light above the folded flowers,

 Till our vicinity
Is rendered royal by their flight
Towards us, till more silently
 The silent stars ignite,
Their aeons dwindling by a night,

 And everything seems bent
On robing in this evening you
And me, all dark the element
 Our light is earnest to,
All quiet gathered round us who,

 When over the embankments
A train that's loudly reprobate
Shoots from silence into silence,
 With ease accommodate
Its pandemonium, its freight.

I hold you close because
We have decided dark will be
For ever like this and because,
  My love, already
The dark is growing elderly.

  With dawn upon its way,
Punctually and as a rule,
The small hours widening into day,
  Our room its vestibule
Before it fills all houses full,

  We too must hazard all,
Switch off the lamp without a word
For the last of night assembled
  Over it and unperturbed
By the moth that lies there littered,

  And notice how the trees
Which took on anonymity
Are again in their huge histories
  Displayed, that wherever we
Attempt, and as far as we can see,

  The flowers everywhere
Are withering, the stars dissolved,
Amalgamated in a glare,
  Which last night were revolved
Discreetly round us – and, involved,

  The two of us, in these
Which early morning has deformed,
Must hope that in new properties
  We'll find a uniform
To know each other truly by, or,

At the least, that these will,
When we rise, be seen with dawn
As remnant yet part raiment still,
    Like flags that linger on
The sky when king and queen are gone.

PERSEPHONE

I

I see as through a skylight in my brain
The mole strew its buildings in the rain,

The swallows turn above their broken home
And all my acres in delirium.

II

Straitjacketed by cold and numskulled
Now sleep the welladjusted and the skilled –

The bat folds its wing like a winter leaf,
The squirrel in its hollow holds aloof.

III

The weasel and ferret, the stoat and fox
Move hand in glove across the equinox.

I can tell how softly their footsteps go –
Their footsteps borrow silence from the snow.

A PERSONAL STATEMENT
for Seamus Heaney

Since you, Mind, think to diagnose
    Experience
As summer, satin, nightingale or rose,
    Of the senses making sense –
      Follow my nose,

Attend all other points of contact,
    Deserve your berth:
My brain-child, help me find my own way back
    To fire, air, water, earth.
      I am, in fact,

More than a bag of skin and bone.
    My person is
A chamber where the elements postpone
    In lively synthesis,
      In peace on loan,

Old wars of flood and earthquake, storm
    And holocaust,
Their attributes most temperately reformed
    Of heatwave and of frost.
      They take my form,

Learn from my arteries their pace –
    They leave alarms
And excursions for my heart and lungs to face.
    I hold them in my arms
      And keep in place.

To walk, to run, to leap, to stand –
        Of the litany
Of movement I the vicar in command,
        The prophet in my country,
            The priest at hand,

Take steps to make it understood
        The occupants
Assembled here in narrow neighbourhood
        Are my constituents
            For bad or good.

Body and Mind, I turn to you.
        It's me you fit.
Whatever you think, whatever you do,
        Include me in on it,
            Essential Two.

Who house philosophy and force,
        Wed well in me
The elements, for fever's their divorce,
        Nightmare and ecstasy,
            And death of course.

My sponsor, Mind, my satellite,
        Keep my balance,
Steer me through my heyday, through my night,
        My senses' common sense,
            Selfcentred light.

And you who set me in my ways,
        Immaculate,
In full possession of my faculties –
        Till you disintegrate,
            Exist to please.

Lest I with fears and hopes capsize,
       By your own lights
Sail, Body, cargoless towards surprise.
       And come, Mind, raise your sights –
          Believe my eyes.

THE OSPREY

To whom certain water talents –
Webbed feet, oils – do not occur,
Regulates his liquid acre
From the sky, his proper element.

There, already, his eye removes
The trout each fathom magnifies.
He lives, without compromise,
His unamphibious two lives –

An inextinguishable bird whom
No lake's waters waterlog.
He shakes his feathers like a dog.
It's all of air that ferries him.

NO CONTINUING CITY

My hands here, gentle, where her breasts begin,
My picture in her eyes –
It is time for me to recognise
This new dimension, my last girl.
So, to set my house in order, I imagine
Photographs, advertisements – the old lies,
The lumber of my soul –

All that is due for spring cleaning,
Everything that soul-destroys.
Into the open I bring
Girls who linger still in photostat
(For whom I was so many different boys) –
I explode their myths before it is too late,
Their promises I detonate –

There is quite a lot that I can do . . .
I leave them – are they six or seven, two or three? –
Locked in their small geographies.
The hillocks of their bodies' lovely shires
(Whose all weathers I have walked through)
Acre by acre recede entire
To summer country.

From collision to eclipse their case is closed.
Who took me by surprise
Like comets first – now, failing to ignite,
They constellate such uneventful skies,
Their stars arranged each night
In the old stories
Which I successfully have diagnosed.

Though they momentarily survive
In my delays,
They neither cancel nor improve
My continuing city with old ways,
Familiar avenues to love –
Down my one-way streets (it is time to finish)
Their eager syllables diminish.

Though they call out from the suburbs
Of experience – they know how that disturbs! –
Or, already tending towards home,
Prepare to hitch-hike on the kerbs,
Their bags full of dear untruths –
I am their medium
And I take the words out of their mouths.

From today new hoardings crowd my eyes,
Pasted over my ancient histories
Which (I must be cruel to be kind)
Only gale or cloudburst now discover,
Ripping the billboard of my mind –
Oh, there my lovers,
There my dead no longer advertise.

I transmit from the heart a closing broadcast
To my girl, my bride, my wife-to-be –
I tell her she is welcome,
Advising her to make this last,
To be sure of finding room in me
(I embody bed and breakfast) –
To eat and drink me out of house and home.

CIRCE

The cries of the shipwrecked enter my head.
On wildest nights when the torn sky confides
Its face to the sea's cracked mirror, my bed
– Addressed by the moon and her tutored tides –

Through brainstorm, through nightmare and ocean
Keeps me afloat. Shallows are my coven,
The comfortable margins – in this notion
I stand uncorrected by the sun even.

Out of the night husband after husband
– Eyes wide as oysters, arms full of driftwood –
Wades ashore and puts in at my island.
My necklaces of sea shells and seaweed,

My skirts of spindrift, sandals of flotsam
Catch the eye of each bridegroom for ever.
Quite forgetful of the widowing calm
My sailors wait through bad and good weather.

At first in rock pools I become their wife,
Under the dunes at last they lie with me –
These are the spring and neap tides of their life.
I have helped so many sailors off the sea,

And, counting no man among my losses,
I have made of my arms and my thighs last rooms
For the irretrievable and capsized –
I extend the sea, its idioms.

FREEZE-UP

The freeze-up annexes the sea even,
Putting out over the waves its platform.
Let skies fall, the fox's belly cave in –
This catastrophic shortlived reform
Directs to our homes the birds of heaven.
They come on farfetched winds to keep us warm.

Bribing these with bounty, we would rather
Forget our hopes of thaw when spring will clean
The boughs, dust from our sills snow and feather,
Release to its decay and true decline
The bittern whom this different weather
Cupboarded in ice like a specimen.

THE HEBRIDES
for Eavan Boland

I

The winds' enclosure, Atlantic's premises,
    Last balconies
  Above the waves, The Hebrides –
    Too long did I postpone
Presbyterian granite and the lack of trees,
    This orphaned stone

Day in, day out colliding with the sea.
    Weather forecast,
  Compass nor ordnance survey
    Arranges my welcome
For, on my own, I have lost my way at last,
    So far from home.

In whom the city is continuing,
    I stop to look,
  To find my feet among the ling
    And bracken – over me
The bright continuum of gulls, a rook
    Occasionally.

II

My eyes, slowly accepting panorama,
    Try to include
  In my original idea
    The total effect
Of air and ocean – waterlogged all wood –
    All harbours wrecked –

My dead-lights latched by whelk and barnacle
    Till I abide
  By the sea wall of the time I kill –
    My each nostalgic scheme
Jettisoned, as crises are, the further side
    Of sleep and dream.

Between wind and wave this holiday
    The cormorant,
  The oystercatcher and osprey
    Proceed and keep in line
While I, hands in my pockets, hesitant,
    Am in two minds.

III

Old neighbours, though shipwreck's my decision,
    People my brain –
  Like breakwaters against the sun,
    Command in silhouette
My island circumstance – my cells retain,
    Perpetuate

Their crumpled deportment through bad weather.
    And I feel them
  Put on their raincoats for ever
    And walk out in the sea.
I am, though each one waves a phantom limb,
    The amputee,

For these are my sailors, these my drowned –
    In their heart of hearts,
  In their city I ran aground.
    Along my arteries
Sluice those homewaters petroleum hurts.
    Dry dock, gantries,

Dykes of apparatus educate my bones
    To track the buoys
  Up sea lanes love emblazons
    To streets where shall conclude
My journey back from flux to poise, from poise
    To attitude.

Here, at the edge of my experience,
    Another tide
  Along the broken shore extends
    A lifetime's wrack and ruin –
No flotsam I may beachcomb now can hide
    That water line.

IV

Beyond the lobster pots where plankton spreads
    Porpoises turn.
  Seals slip over the cockle beds.
    Undertow dishevels
Seaweed in the shallows – and I discern
    My sea levels.

To right and left of me there intervene
    The tumbled burns –
  And these, on turf and boulder weaned,
    Confuse my calendar –
Their tilt is suicidal, their great return
    Curricular.

No matter what repose holds shore and sky
    In harmony,
  From this place in the long run I,
    Though here I might have been
Content with rivers where they meet the sea,
    Remove upstream,

Where the salmon, risking fastest waters –
    Waterfall and rock
  And the effervescent otters –
    On bridal pools insist
As with fin and generation they unlock
    The mountain's fist.

V

Now, buttoned up, with water in my shoes,
    Clouds around me,
  I can, through mist that misconstrues,
    Read like a palimpsest
My past – those landmarks and that scenery
    I dare resist.

Into my mind's unsympathetic trough
    They fade away –
  And to alter my perspective
    I feel in the sharp cold
Of my vantage point too high above the bay
    The sea grow old.

Granting the trawlers far below their stance,
    Their anchorage,
  I fight all the way for balance –
    In the mountain's shadow
Losing foothold, covet the privilege
    Of vertigo.

ELEGY FOR FATS WALLER

Lighting up, lest all our hearts should break,
His fiftieth cigarette of the day,
Happy with so many notes at his beck
And call, he sits there taking it away,
The maker of immaculate slapstick.

With music and with such precise rampage
Across the deserts of the blues a trail
He blazes, towards the one true mirage,
Enormous on a nimble-footed camel
And almost refusing to be his age.

He plays for hours on end and though there be
Oases one part water, two parts gin,
He tumbles past to reign, wise and thirsty,
At the still centre of his loud dominion –
THE SHOOK THE SHAKE THE SHEIKH OF ARABY.

IN MEMORIAM

My father, let no similes eclipse
Where crosses like some forest simplified
Sink roots into my mind; the slow sands
Of your history delay till through your eyes
I read you like a book. Before you died,
Re-enlisting with all the broken soldiers
You bent beneath your rucksack, near collapse,
In anecdote rehearsed and summarised
These words I write in memory. Let yours
And other heartbreaks play into my hands.

Now I see in close-up, in my mind's eye,
The cracked and splintered dead for pity's sake
Each dismal evening predecease the sun,
You, looking death and nightmare in the face
With your kilt, harmonica and gun,
Grow older in a flash, but none the wiser
(Who, following the wrong queue at The Palace,
Have joined the London Scottish by mistake),
Your nineteen years uncertain if and why
Belgium put the kibosh on the Kaiser.

Between the corpses and the soup canteens
You swooned away, watching your future spill.
But, as it was, your proper funeral urn
Had mercifully smashed to smithereens,
To shrapnel shards that sliced your testicle.
That instant I, your most unlikely son,
In No Man's Land was surely left for dead,
Blotted out from your far horizon.
As your voice now is locked inside my head,
I yet was held secure, waiting my turn.

Finally, that lousy war was over.
Stranded in France and in need of proof
You hunted down experimental lovers,
Persuading chorus girls and countesses:
This, father, the last confidence you spoke.
In my twentieth year your old wounds woke
As cancer. Lodging under the same roof
Death was a visitor who hung about,
Strewing the house with pills and bandages,
Till he chose to put your spirit out.

Though they overslept the sequence of events
Which ended with the ambulance outside,
You lingering in the hall, your bowels on fire,
Tears in your eyes, and all your medals spent,
I summon girls who packed at last and went
Underground with you. Their souls again on hire,
Now those lost wives as recreated brides
Take shape before me, materialise.
On the verge of light and happy legend
They lift their skirts like blinds across your eyes.

LEAVING INISHMORE

Rain and sunlight and the boat between them
Shifted whole hillsides through the afternoon –
Quiet variations on an urgent theme
Reminding me now that we left too soon
The island awash in wave and anthem.

Miles from the brimming enclave of the bay
I hear again the Atlantic's voices,
The gulls above us as we pulled away –
So munificent their final noises
These are the broadcasts from our holiday.

Oh, the crooked walkers on that tilting floor!
And the girls singing on the upper deck
Whose hair took the light like a downpour –
Interim nor change of scene shall shipwreck
Those folk on the move between shore and shore.

Summer and solstice as the seasons turn
Anchor our boat in a perfect standstill,
The harbour wall of Inishmore astern
Where the Atlantic waters overspill –
I shall name this the point of no return

Lest that excursion out of light and heat
Take on a January idiom –
Our ocean icebound when the year is hurt,
Wintertime past cure – the curriculum
Vitae of sailors and the sick at heart.

JOURNEY OUT OF ESSEX
or, John Clare's Escape from the Madhouse

I am lying with my head
Over the edge of the world,
Unpicking my whereabouts
Like the asylum's name
That they stitch on the sheets.

Sick now with bad weather
Or a virus from the fens,
I dissolve in a puddle
My biographies of birds
And the names of flowers.

That they may recuperate
Alongside the stunned mouse,
The hedgehog rolled in leaves,
I am putting to bed
In this rheumatic ditch

The boughs of my harvest-home,
My wives, one on either side,
And keeping my head low as
A lark's nest, my feet toward
Helpston and the pole star.

CARAVAN

A rickety chimney suggests
The diminutive stove,
Children perhaps, the pots
And pans adding up to love –

So much concentrated under
The low roof, the windows
Shuttered against snow and wind,
That you would be magnified

(If you were there) by the dark,
Wearing it like an apron
And revolving in your hands
As weather in a glass dome,

The blizzard, the day beyond
And – tiny, barely in focus –
Me disappearing out of view
On probably the only horse,

Cantering off to the right
To collect the week's groceries,
Or to be gone for good
Having drawn across my eyes

Like a curtain all that light
And the snow, my history
Stiffening with the tea towels
Hung outside the door to dry.

SWANS MATING

Even now I wish that you had been there
Sitting beside me on the riverbank:
The cob and his pen sailing in rhythm
Until their small heads met and the final
Heraldic moment dissolved in ripples.

This was a marriage and a baptism,
A holding of breath, nearly a drowning,
Wings spread wide for balance where he trod,
Her feathers full of water and her neck
Under the water like a bar of light.

GALAPAGOS

Now you have scattered into islands –
Breasts, belly, knees, the mount of Venus,
Each a Galapagos of the mind
Where you, the perfect stranger, prompter
Of throw-backs, of hold-ups in time,

Embody peculiar animals –
The giant tortoise hesitating,
The shy lemur, the iguana's
Slow gaze in which the *Beagle* anchors
With its homesick scientist on board.

BADGER
for Raymond Piper

I

Pushing the wedge of his body
Between cromlech and stone circle,
He excavates down mine shafts
And back into the depths of the hill.

His path straight and narrow
And not like the fox's zig-zags,
The arc of the hare who leaves
A silhouette on the sky line.

Night's silence around his shoulders,
His face lit by the moon, he
Manages the earth with his paws,
Returns underground to die.

II

An intestine taking in
patches of dog's-mercury,
brambles, the bluebell wood;
a heel revolving acorns;
a head with a price on it
brushing cuckoo-spit, goose-grass;
a name that parishes borrow.

III

For the digger, the earth-dog
It is a difficult delivery
Once the tongs take hold,

Vulnerable his pig's snout
That lifted cow-pats for beetles,
Hedgehogs for the soft meat,

His limbs dragging after them
So many stones turned over,
The trees they tilted.

CASUALTY

Its decline was gradual,
A sequence of explorations
By other animals, each
Looking for the easiest way in –

A surgical removal of the eyes,
A probing of the orifices,
Bitings down through the skin,
Through tracts where the grasses melt,

And the bad air released
In a ceremonious wounding
So slow that more and more
I wanted to get closer to it.

A candid grin, the bones
Accumulating to a diagram
Except for the polished horns,
The immaculate hooves.

And this no final reduction
For the ribs began to scatter,
The wool to move outward
As though hunger still worked there,

As though something that had followed
Fox and crow was desperate for
A last morsel and was
Other than the wind or rain.

READINGS
for Peter Longley

I

I remember your eyes in bandages
And me reading to you like a mother;
Our grubby redeemer, the chimney-sweep
Whose baptism among the seaweed
Began when he stopped astounded beside
The expensive bed, the white coverlet,
The most beautiful girl he had ever seen –
Her hair on the eiderdown like algae,
Her face a reflection in clean water;
The Irishwoman haunting Tom's shoulder –
The shawl's canopy, the red petticoats
Arriving beside him again and again,
The white feet accompanying his feet,
All of the leafy roads down to the sea.

II

Other faces at the frosty window,
Kay and Gerda in their separate attics;
The icicle driven into Kay's heart –
Then a glance at the pillow where you
Twisted your head again and tried to squeeze
Light like a tear through the bandages.

from LETTERS

To Derek Mahon

And did we come into our own
When, minus muse and lexicon,
We traced in August sixty-nine
Our imaginary Peace Line
Around the burnt-out houses of
The Catholics we'd scarcely loved,
Two Sisyphuses come to budge
The sticks and stones of an old grudge,

Two poetic conservatives
In the city of guns and long knives,
Our ears receiving then and there
The stereophonic nightmare
Of the Shankill and the Falls,
Our matches struck on crumbling walls
To light us as we moved at last
Through the back alleys of Belfast?

Why it mattered to have you here
You who journeyed to Inisheer
With me, years back, one Easter when
With MacIntyre and the lone Dane
Our footsteps lifted up the larks
Echoing off those western rocks
And down that darkening arcade
Hung with the failures of our trade,

Will understand. We were tongue-tied
Companions of the island's dead
In the graveyard among the dunes,
Eavesdroppers on conversations
With a Jesus who spoke Irish –
We were strangers in that parish,
Black tea with bacon and cabbage
For our sacraments and pottage,

Dank blankets making up our Lent
Till, islanders ourselves, we bent
Our knees and cut the watery sod
From the lazy-bed where slept a God
We couldn't count among our friends,
Although we'd taken in our hands
Splinters of driftwood nailed and stuck
On the rim of the Atlantic.

That was Good Friday years ago –
How persistent the undertow
Slapped by currachs ferrying stones,
Moonlight glossing the confusions
Of its each bilingual wave – yes,
We would have lingered there for less . . .
Six islanders for a ten-bob note
Rowed us out to the anchored boat.

To Seamus Heaney

From Carrigskeewaun in Killadoon
I write, although I'll see you soon,
Hoping this fortnight detonates
Your year in the United States,
Offering you by way of welcome
To the sick counties we call home
The mystical point at which I tire
Of Calor gas and a turf fire.

Till we talk again in Belfast
Pleasanter far to leave the past
Across three acres and two brooks
On holiday in a post box
Which dripping fuchsia bells surround,
Its back to the prevailing wind,
And where sanderlings from Iceland
Court the breakers, take my stand,

Disinfecting with a purer air
That small subconscious cottage where
The Irish poet slams his door
On slow-worm, toad and adder:
Beneath these racing skies it is
A tempting stance indeed – *ipsis*
Hibernicis Hiberniores –
Except that we know the old stories,

The midden of cracked hurley sticks
Tied to recall the crucifix,
Of broken bones and lost scruples,
The blackened hearth, the blazing gable's
Telltale cinder where we may
Scorch our shins until that day
We sleepwalk through a No Man's Land
Lipreading to an Orange band.

Continually, therefore, we rehearse
Goodbyes to all our characters
And, since both would have it both ways,
On the oily roll of calmer seas
Launch coffin-ship and life-boat,
Body with soul thus kept afloat,
Mind open like a half-door
To the speckled hill, the plovers' shore.

So let it be the lapwing's cry
That lodges in the throat as I
Raise its alarum from the mud,
Seeking for your sake to conclude
Ulster Poet our Union Title
And prolong this sad recital
By leaving careful footprints round
A wind-encircled burial mound.

WOUNDS

Here are two pictures from my father's head –
I have kept them like secrets until now:
First, the Ulster Division at the Somme
Going over the top with 'Fuck the Pope!'
'No Surrender!': a boy about to die,
Screaming 'Give 'em one for the Shankill!'
'Wilder than Gurkhas' were my father's words
Of admiration and bewilderment.
Next comes the London-Scottish padre
Resettling kilts with his swagger-stick,
With a stylish backhand and a prayer.
Over a landscape of dead buttocks
My father followed him for fifty years.
At last, a belated casualty,
He said – lead traces flaring till they hurt –
'I am dying for King and Country, slowly.'
I touched his hand, his thin head I touched.

Now, with military honours of a kind,
With his badges, his medals like rainbows,
His spinning compass, I bury beside him
Three teenage soldiers, bellies full of
Bullets and Irish beer, their flies undone.
A packet of Woodbines I throw in,
A lucifer, the Sacred Heart of Jesus
Paralysed as heavy guns put out
The night-light in a nursery for ever;
Also a bus-conductor's uniform –
He collapsed beside his carpet-slippers
Without a murmur, shot through the head
By a shivering boy who wandered in
Before they could turn the television down
Or tidy away the supper dishes.
To the children, to a bewildered wife,
I think 'Sorry Missus' was what he said.

CARRIGSKEEWAUN
for Penny & David Cabot

The Mountain

This is ravens' territory, skulls, bones,
The marrow of these boulders supervised
From the upper air: I stand alone here
And seem to gather children about me,
A collection of picnic things, my voice
Filling the district as I call their names.

The Path

With my first step I dislodge the mallards
Whose necks strain over the bog to where
Kittiwakes scrape the waves: then, the circle
Widening, lapwings, curlews, snipe until
I am left with only one swan to nudge
To the far side of its gradual disdain.

The Strand

I discover, remaindered from yesterday,
Cattle tracks, a sanderling's tiny trail,
The footprints of the children and my own
Linking the dunes to the water's edge,
Reducing to sand the dry shells, the toe-
And fingernail parings of the sea.

The Wall

I join all the men who have squatted here
This lichened side of the drystone wall
And notice how smoke from our turf fire
Recalls in the cool air above the lake
Steam from a kettle, a tablecloth and
A table she might have already set.

The Lake

Though it will duplicate at any time
The sheep and cattle that wander there,
For a few minutes every evening
Its surface seems tilted to receive
The sun perfectly, the mare and her foal,
The heron, all such special visitors.

THE WEST

Beneath a gas-mantle that the moths bombard,
Light that powders at a touch, dusty wings,
I listen for news through the atmospherics,
A crackle of sea-wrack, spinning driftwood,
Waves like distant traffic, news from home,

Or watch myself, as through a sandy lens,
Materialising out of the heat-shimmers
And finding my way for ever along
The path to this cottage, its windows,
Walls, sun and moon dials, home from home.

IN MEMORY OF GERARD DILLON

I

You walked, all of a sudden, through
The rickety gate which opens
To a scatter of curlews,
An acre of watery light; your grave
A dip in the dunes where sand mislays
The sound of the sea, earth over you
Like a low Irish sky; the sun
An electric light bulb clouded
By the sandy tides, sunlight lost
And found, a message in a bottle.

II

You are a room full of self-portraits,
A face that follows us everywhere;
An ear to the ground listening for
Dead brothers in layers; an eye
Taking in the beautiful predators –
Cats on the windowsill, birds of prey
And, between the diminutive fields,
A dragonfly, wings full of light
Where the road narrows to the last farm.

III

Christening robes, communion dresses,
The shawls of factory workers,
A blind drawn on the Lower Falls.

SKARA BRAE
for Sheila & Denis Smyth

A window into the ground,
The bumpy lawn in section,
An exploded view
Through middens, through lives,

The thatch of grass roots,
The gravelly roof compounding
Periwinkles, small bones,
A calendar of meals,

The thread between sepulchre
And home a broken necklace,
Knuckles, dice scattering
At the warren's core,

Pebbles the tide washes
That conceded for so long
Living room, the hard beds,
The table made of stone.

ALIBIS

I

My botanical studies took me among
Those whom I now consider my ancestors.
I used to appear to them at odd moments –
With buckets of water in the distance, or
At the campfire, my arms full of snowy sticks.
Beech mast, hedgehogs, cresses were my diet,
My medicaments badger grease and dock leaves.
A hard life. Nevertheless, they named after me
A clover that flourished on those distant slopes.
Later I found myself playing saxophone
On the Souza Band's Grand Tour of the World.
Perhaps because so much was happening
I started, in desperation, to keep a diary.
(I have no idea what came over me.)
After that I sat near a sunny window
Waiting for pupils among the music-stands.
At present I am drafting appendices
To lost masterpieces, some of them my own –
Requiems, entertainments for popes and kings.
From time to time I choose to express myself
In this manner, the basic line. Indeed,
My one remaining ambition is to be
The last poet in Europe to find a rhyme.

II

I wanted this to be a lengthy meditation
With myself as the central character –
Official guide through the tall pavilions
Or even the saviour of damaged birds.
I accepted my responsibilities
And was managing daily after matins
And before lunch my stint of composition.
But gradually, as though I had planned it,

And with only a few more pages to go
Of my *Apologia Pro Vita Mea*,
There dawned on me this idea of myself
Clambering aboard an express train full of
Honeymoon couples and football supporters.
I had folded my life like a cheque book,
Wrapped my pyjamas around two noggins
To keep, for a while at least, my visions warm.
Tattered and footloose in my final phase
I improvised on the map of the world
And hurtled to join, among the police files,
My obstreperous bigfisted brothers.

III

I could always have kept myself to myself
And, falling asleep with the light still on,
Reached the quiet conclusion that this
(And this is where I came in) was no more than
The accommodation of different weathers,
Whirlwind tours around the scattered islands,
Telephone calls from the guilty suburbs,
From the back of the mind, a simple question
Of being in two places at the one time.

OPTIONS
for Michael Allen

Ha! here's three on 's are sophisticated.
Thou art the thing itself.

These were my options: firstly
To have gone on and on –
A garrulous correspondence
Between me, the ideal reader
And – a halo to high-light
My head – that outer circle
Of critical intelligences
Deciphering – though with telling
Lacunae – my life-story,
Holding up to the bright mirrors
Of expensive libraries
My candours in palimpsest,
My collected blotting papers.

Or, at a pinch, I could have
Implied in reduced haiku
A world of suffering, swaddled
In white silence like babies
The rows of words, the mono-
Syllabic titles – my brain sore
And, as I struggled to master
The colon, my poet's tongue
Scorched by nicotine and coffee,
By the voracious acids
Of my *Ars Poetica*,
My clenched fist – towards midnight –
A paperweight on the language.

Or a species of skinny stanza
Might have materialised
In laborious versions
After the Finnish, for epigraph
The wry juxtaposing of
Wise-cracks by Groucho or Mae West
And the hushed hexameters
Of the right pastoral poet
From the Silver Age – Bacchylides
For instance – the breathings reversed,
The accents wrong mostly – proof,
If such were needed, of my humour
Among the big dictionaries.

These were my options, I say –
Night-lights, will-o'-the-wisps
Out of bog-holes and dark corners
Pointing towards the asylum
Where, for a quid of tobacco
Or a snatch of melody,
I might have cut off my head
In so many words – to borrow
A diagnosis of John Clare's –
Siphoning through the ears
Letters of the alphabet
And, with the vowels and consonants,
My life of make-believe.

THE LODGER

The lodger is writing a novel.
We give him the run of the house
But he occupies my mind as well –
An attic, a lumber-room
For his typewriter, notebooks,
The slowly accumulating pages.

At the end of each four-fingered
Suffering line the angelus rings –
A hundred noons and sunsets
As we lie here whispering,
Careful not to curtail our lives
Or change the names he has given us.

THE BAT

We returned to the empty ballroom
And found a bat demented there, quite
Out of its mind, flashing round and round
Where earlier the dancers had moved.

We opened a window and shouted
To jam the signals and, so we thought,
Inspire a tangent in the tired skull,
A swerve, a saving miscalculation.

We had come to make love secretly
Without disturbance or obstacle,
And fell like shadows across the bat's
Singlemindedness, sheer insanity.

I told you of the blind snake that thrives
In total darkness by eating bats,
Of centuries measured in bat droppings,
The light bones that fall out of the air.

You called it a sky-mouse and described
Long fingers, anaesthetising teeth,
How it clung to the night by its thumbs,
And suggested that we leave it there.

Suspended between floor and ceiling
It would continue in our absence
And drop exhausted, a full stop
At the centre of the ballroom floor.

IN MAYO

I

For her sake once again I disinter
Imagination like a brittle skull
From where the separating vertebrae
And scapulae litter a sandy wind,

As though to reach her I must circle
This burial mound, its shadow turning
Under the shadow of a seabird's wing:
A sundial for the unhallowed soul.

II

Though the townland's all ears, all eyes
To decipher our movements, she and I
Appear on the scene at the oddest times:
We follow the footprints of animals,

Then vanish into the old wives' tales
Leaving behind us landmarks to be named
After our episodes, and the mushrooms
That cluster where we happen to lie.

III

When it is time for her to fall asleep
And I touch her eyelids, may night itself,
By my rule of thumb, be no profounder
Than the grassy well among irises

Where wild duck shelter their candid eggs:
No more beguiling than a gull's feather
In whose manifold gradations of light
I clothe her now and erase the scene.

IV

Dawns and dusks here should consist of
Me scooping a hollow for her hip-bone,
The stony headland a bullaun, a cup
To balance her body in like water:

Then a slow awakening to the swans
That fly home in twos, married for life,
Larks nestling beside the cattle's feet
And snipe the weight of the human soul.

LANDSCAPE

Here my imagination
Tangles through a turfstack
Like skeins of sheep's wool:
Is a bull's horn silting
With powdery seashells.

I am clothed, unclothed
By racing cloud shadows,
Or else disintegrate
Like a hillside neighbour
Erased by sea mist.

A place of dispersals
Where the wind fractures
Flight-feathers, insect wings
And rips thought to tatters
Like a fuchsia petal.

For seconds, dawn or dusk,
The sun's at an angle
To read inscriptions by:
The splay of the badger
And the otter's skidmarks

Melting into water
Where a minnow flashes:
A mouth drawn to a mouth
Digests the glass between
Me and my reflection.

WEATHER

I carry indoors
Two circles of blue sky,
Splinters of sunlight
As spring water tilts
And my buckets, heavy

Under the pressure of
Enormous atmospheres,
Two lakes and the islands
Enlarging constantly,
Tug at my shoulders, or,

With a wet sky low as
The ceiling, I shelter
Landmarks, keep track of
Animals, all the birds
In a reduced outdoors

And open my windows,
The wings of dragonflies
Hung from an alder cone,
A raindrop enclosing
Brookweed's five petals.

HALCYON

Grandmother's plumage was death
To the few remaining grebes,
The solitary kingfisher
That haunted a riverbank.

But, then, I consider her
The last of the Pearly Queens
To walk under tall feathers –
The trophies of sweethearts

Who aimed from leafy towpaths
Pistols, silver bullets,
Or sank among bulrushes
Laying out nets of silk.

So many trigger fingers
And hands laid upon water
Should let materialise
A bird that breeds in winter,

That settles bad weather,
The winds of sickness and death –
Halcyon to the ancients
And kingfisher in those days,

Though perhaps even she knew
It was the eccentric grebe
Whose feet covered the surface,
Whose nest floated on the waves.

STILTS
for Paul Muldoon

Two grandfathers sway on stilts
Past my bedroom window.
They should be mending holes
In the Big Top, but that would be
Like putting out the stars.

The first has been a teacher
Of ballroom dancing, but now
Abandons house and home
To lift in the Grand Parade
High knees above the neighbours.

The second, a carpenter,
Comes from another town
With tools and material
To manufacture stilts
And playthings for the soul.

MASTER OF CEREMONIES

My grandfather, a natural master of ceremonies
('Boys! Girls! Take your partners for the Military Two-step!')
Had thrown out his only son, my sad retarded uncle
Who, good for nothing except sleepwalking to the Great War,
Was not once entrusted with rifle or bayonet but instead
Went over the top slowly behind the stretcher parties
And, as park attendant where all hell had broken loose,
Collected littered limbs until his sack was heavy.
In old age my grandfather demoted his flesh and blood
And over the cribbage board ('Fifteen two, fifteen four,
One for his nob') would call me Lionel. 'Sorry. My mistake.
That was my nephew. His head got blown off in No Man's Land.'

EDWARD THOMAS'S WAR DIARY
1 January – 8 April, 1917

One night in the trenches
You dreamed you were at home
And couldn't stay to tea,
Then woke where shell holes
Filled with bloodstained water,

Where empty beer bottles
Littered the barbed wire – still
Wondering why there sang
No thrushes in all that
Hazel, ash and dogwood,

Your eye on what remained –
Light spangling through a hole
In the cathedral wall
And the little conical
Summer house among trees.

Green feathers of yarrow
Were just fledging the sods
Of your dugout when you
Skirted the danger zone
To draw panoramas,

To receive larks singing
Like a letter from home
Posted in No Man's Land
Where one frantic bat seemed
A piece of burnt paper.

FLEANCE

I entered with a torch before me
And cast my shadow on the backcloth
Momentarily: a handful of words,
One bullet with my initials on it –
And that got stuck in a property tree.

I would have caught it between my teeth
Or, a true professional, stood still
While the two poetic murderers
Pinned my silhouette to history
In a shower of accurate daggers.

But as any illusionist might
Unfasten the big sack of darkness,
The ropes and handcuffs, and emerge
Smoking a nonchalant cigarette,
I escaped – only to lose myself.

It took me a lifetime to explore
The dusty warren beneath the stage
With its trapdoor opening on to
All that had happened above my head
Like noises-off or distant weather.

In the empty auditorium I bowed
To one preoccupied caretaker
And, without removing my make-up,
Hurried back to the digs where Banquo
Sat up late with a hole in his head.

COMPANY

I imagine a day when the children
Are drawers full of soft toys, photographs
Beside the only surviving copies
Of the books that summarise my lifetime,
And I have begun to look forward to
Retirement, second childhood, except that
Love has diminished to one high room
Below which the vigilantes patrol
While I attempt to make myself heard
Above the cacophonous plumbing, and you
Who are my solitary interpreter
Can bear my company for long enough
To lipread such fictions as I believe
Will placate remote customs officials,
The border guards, or even reassure
Anxious butchers, greengrocers, tradesmen
On whom we depend for our daily bread,
The dissemination of manuscripts,
News from the outside world, simple acts
Of such unpatriotic generosity
That until death we hesitate together
On the verge of an almost total silence:

Or else we are living in the country
In a far-off townland divided by
The distances it takes to overhear
A quarrel or the sounds of love-making,
Where even impoverished households
Can afford to focus binoculars
On our tiny windows, the curtains
That wear my motionless silhouette
As I sit late beside a tilley-lamp
And try to put their district on the map

And to name the fields for them, for you
Who busy yourself about the cottage,
Its thatch letting in, the tall grasses
And the rain leaning against the half-door,
Dust on the rafters and our collection
Of curious utensils, pots and pans
The only escape from which is the twice
Daily embarrassed journey to and from
The well we have choked with alder branches
For the cattle's safety, their hoofprints
A thirsty circle in the puddles,
Watermarks under all that we say.

MAN LYING ON A WALL
Homage to L. S. Lowry

You could draw a straight line from the heels,
Through calves, buttocks and shoulder-blades
To the back of the head: pressure points
That bear the enormous weight of the sky.
Should you take away the supporting structure
The result would be a miracle or
An extremely clever conjuring trick.
As it is, the man lying on the wall
Is wearing the serious expression
Of popes and kings in their final slumber,
His deportment not dissimilar to
Their stiff, reluctant exits from this world
Above the shoulders of the multitude.

It is difficult to judge whether or not
He is sleeping or merely disinclined
To arrive punctually at the office
Or to return home in time for his tea.
He is wearing a pinstripe suit, black shoes
And a bowler hat: on the pavement
Below him, like a relic or something
He is trying to forget, his briefcase
With everybody's initials on it.

WREATHS

The Civil Servant

He was preparing an Ulster Fry for breakfast
When someone walked into the kitchen and shot him:
A bullet entered his mouth and pierced his skull,
The books he had read, the music he could play.

He lay in his dressing gown and pyjamas
While they dusted the dresser for fingerprints
And then shuffled backwards across the garden
With notebooks, cameras and measuring tapes.

They rolled him up like a red carpet and left
Only a bullet hole in the cutlery drawer:
Later his widow took a hammer and chisel
And removed the black keys from his piano.

The Greengrocer

He ran a good shop, and he died
Serving even the death-dealers
Who found him busy as usual
Behind the counter, organised
With holly wreaths for Christmas,
Fir trees on the pavement outside.

Astrologers or three wise men
Who may shortly be setting out
For a small house up the Shankill
Or the Falls, should pause on their way
To buy gifts at Jim Gibson's shop,
Dates and chestnuts and tangerines.

The Linen Workers

Christ's teeth ascended with him into heaven:
Through a cavity in one of his molars
The wind whistles: he is fastened for ever
By his exposed canines to a wintry sky.

I am blinded by the blaze of that smile
And by the memory of my father's false teeth
Brimming in their tumbler: they wore bubbles
And, outside of his body, a deadly grin.

When they massacred the ten linen workers
There fell on the road beside them spectacles,
Wallets, small change, and a set of dentures:
Blood, food particles, the bread, the wine.

Before I can bury my father once again
I must polish the spectacles, balance them
Upon his nose, fill his pockets with money
And into his dead mouth slip the set of teeth.

SECOND SIGHT

My father's mother had the second sight.
Flanders began at the kitchen window –
The mangle rusting in No Man's Land, gas
Turning the antimacassars yellow
When it blew the wrong way from the salient.

In bandages, on crutches, reaching home
Before his letters, my father used to find
The front door on the latch, his bed airing.
'I watched my son going over the top.
He was carrying flowers out of the smoke.'

I have brought the *Pocket Guide to London,*
My *Map of the Underground,* an address –
A lover looking for somewhere to live,
A ghost among ghosts of aunts and uncles
Who crowd around me to give directions.

Where is my father's house, where my father?
If I could walk in on my grandmother
She'd see right through me and the hallway
And the miles of cloud and sky to Ireland.
'You have crossed the water to visit me.'

SPRING TIDE

I

I seem lower than the distant waves,
Their roar diluting to the stillness
Of the sea's progression across these flats,
A map of water so adjusted
It behaves like a preservative
And erases neither the cattle's
And the sheep's nor my own footprints.
I leave hieroglyphics under glass
As well as feathers that hardly budge,
Down abandoned at preening places
That last so long as grassy islands
Where swans unravel among the ferns.

II

It isn't really a burial mound
Reflected there, but all that remains
Of a sandy meadow, a graveyard
Where it was easy to dig the graves.
The spring tide circles and excavates
A shrunken ramshackle pyramid
Rinsing cleaner scapulae, tibias,
Loose teeth, cowrie and nautilus shells
Before seeping after sun and moon
To pour cupfuls into the larks' nests,
To break a mirror on the grazing
And lift minnows over the low bridge.

III

The spring tide has ferried jelly fish
To the end of the lane, pinks, purples,
Wet flowers beside the floating cow-pats.
The zig-zags I make take me among
White cresses and brookweed, lousewort,
Water plantain and grass of parnassus
With engraved capillaries, ivory sheen:
By a drystone wall in the dune slack
The greenish sepals, the hidden blush
And a lip's red veins and yellow spots –
Marsh helleborine waiting for me
To come and go with the spring tide.

ASH KEYS

Ghosts of hedgers and ditchers,
The ash trees rattling keys
Above tangles of hawthorn
And bramble, alder and gorse,

Would keep me from pacing
Commonage, long perspectives
And conversations, a field
That touches the horizon.

I am herding cattle there
As a boy, as the old man
Following in his footsteps
Who begins the task again,

As though there'd never been
In some interim or hollow
Wives and children, milk
And buttermilk, market days.

Far from the perimeter
Of watercress and berries,
In the middle of the field
I stand talking to myself,

While the ash keys scatter
And the gates creak open
And the barbed wire rusts
To hay-ropes strung with thorns.

FROZEN RAIN

I slow down the waterfall to a chandelier,
Filaments of daylight, bones fleshed out by ice
That recuperate in their bandages of glass
And, where the lake behaves like a spirit-level,
I save pockets of air for the otter to breathe.

I magnify each individual blade of grass
With frozen rain, a crop of icicles and twigs,
Fingers and thumbs that beckon towards the thaw
And melt to the marrow between lip and tongue
While the wind strikes the branches like a celeste.

THAW

Snow curls into the coalhouse, flecks the coal.
We burn the snow as well in bad weather
As though to spring-clean that darkening hole.
The thaw's a blackbird with one white feather.

Brothers

I was a mother and a father to him
Once his pebble spectacles had turned cloudy
And his walk slowed to a chair by the fire.
Often I would come back from herding sheep
Or from the post office with our pensions
To find his darkness in darkness, the turf
Shifting ashes on to last flakes of light.
The room was made more silent by the flies
That circled the soup stains on his waistcoat.
The dog preferred to curl up under his hand
And raced ahead as soon as I neared the lane.
I read to him from one of his six books,
Thick pages dropping from the broken spines
Of *Westward Ho!* and *The Children's Reciter.*
Sometimes I pulled faces, and he didn't know,
Or I paraded naked in front of him
As though I was looking in a mirror.
Two neighbours came visiting after he died.
Mad for the learning, a character, they said
And awakened in me a pride of sorts.
I picture his hand when I stroke the dog,
His legs if I knock the kettle from the hearth.
It's his peculiar way of putting things
That fills in the spaces of Thallabaun.
The dregs stewed in the teapot remind me,
And wind creaming rainwater off the butt.

Self-heal

I wanted to teach him the names of flowers,
Self-heal and centaury; on the long acre
Where cattle never graze, bog asphodel.
Could I love someone so gone in the head
And, as they say, was I leading him on?
He'd slept in the cot until he was twelve
Because of his babyish ways, I suppose,
Or the lack of a bed: hadn't his father
Gambled away all but rushy pasture?
His skull seemed to be hammered like a wedge
Into his shoulders, and his back was hunched,
Which gave him an almost scholarly air.
But he couldn't remember the things I taught:
Each name would hover above its flower
Like a butterfly unable to alight.
That day I pulled a cuckoo-pint apart
To release the giddy insects from their cell.
Gently he slipped his hand between my thighs.
I wasn't frightened; and still I don't know why,
But I ran from him in tears to tell them.
I heard how every day for one whole week
He was flogged with a blackthorn, then tethered
In the hayfield. I might have been the cow
Whose tail he would later dock with shears,
And he the ram tangled in barbed wire
That he stoned to death when they set him free.

PEACE
after Tibullus

Who was responsible for the very first arms deal –
The man of iron who thought of marketing the sword?
Or did he intend us to use it against wild animals
Rather than ourselves? Even if he's not guilty
Murder got into the bloodstream as gene or virus
So that now we give birth to wars, short cuts to death.
Blame the affluent society: no killings when
The cup on the dinner table was made of beechwood,
And no barricades or ghettos when the shepherd
Snoozed among sheep that weren't even thoroughbreds.

I would like to have been alive in the good old days
Before the horrors of modern warfare and warcries
Stepping up my pulse rate. Alas, as things turn out
I've been press-ganged into service, and for all I know
Someone's polishing a spear with my number on it.
God of my Fathers, look after me like a child!
And don't be embarrassed by this handmade statue
Carved out of bog oak by my great-great-grandfather
Before the mass-production of religious art
When a wooden god stood simply in a narrow shrine.

A man could worship there with bunches of early grapes,
A wreath of whiskery wheat-ears, and then say Thank you
With a wholemeal loaf delivered by him in person,
His daughter carrying the unbroken honeycomb.
If the good Lord keeps me out of the firing line
I'll pick a porker from the steamy sty and dress
In my Sunday best, a country cousin's sacrifice.
Someone else can slaughter enemy commanders
And, over a drink, rehearse with me his memoirs,
Mapping the camp in wine upon the table top.

It's crazy to beg black death to join the ranks
Who dogs our footsteps anyhow with silent feet –
No cornfields in Hell, nor cultivated vineyards,
Only yapping Cerberus and the unattractive
Oarsman of the Styx: there an anaemic crew
Sleepwalks with smoky hair and empty eye-sockets.
How much nicer to have a family and let
Lazy old age catch up on you in your retirement,
You keeping track of the sheep, your son of the lambs,
While the woman of the house puts on the kettle.

I want to live until the white hairs shine above
A pensioner's memories of better days. Meanwhile
I would like peace to be my partner on the farm,
Peace personified: oxen under the curved yoke;
Compost for the vines, grape-juice turning into wine,
Vintage years handed down from father to son;
Hoe and ploughshare gleaming, while in some dark corner
Rust keeps the soldier's grisly weapons in their place;
The labourer steering his wife and children home
In a hay cart from the fields, a trifle sozzled.

Then, if there are skirmishes, guerrilla tactics,
It's only lovers quarrelling, the bedroom door
Wrenched off its hinges, a woman in hysterics,
Hair torn out, cheeks swollen with bruises and tears –
Until the bully-boy starts snivelling as well
In a pang of conscience for his battered wife:
Then sexual neurosis works them up again
And the row escalates into a war of words.
He's hard as nails, made of sticks and stones, the chap
Who beats his girlfriend up. A crime against nature.

Enough, surely, to rip from her skin the flimsiest
Of negligees, ruffle that elaborate hair-do,
Enough to be the involuntary cause of tears –
Though upsetting a sensitive girl when you sulk
Is a peculiar satisfaction. But punch-ups,
Physical violence, are out: you might as well
Pack your kit-bag, goose-step a thousand miles away
From the female sex. As for me, I want a woman
To come and fondle my ears of wheat and let apples
Overflow between her breasts. I shall call her Peace.

THE WAR POETS

Unmarked were the bodies of the soldier-poets
For shrapnel opened up again the fontanel
Like a hailstone melting towards deep water
At the bottom of a well, or a mosquito
Balancing its tiny shadow above the lip.

It was rushes of air that took the breath away
As though curtains were drawn suddenly aside
And darkness streamed into the dormitory
Where everybody talked about the war ending
And always it would be the last week of the war.

BOG COTTON

Let me make room for bog cotton, a desert flower –
Keith Douglas, I nearly repeat what you were saying
When you apostrophised the poppies of Flanders
And the death of poetry there: that was in Egypt
Among the sandy soldiers of another war.

(It hangs on by a thread, denser than thistledown,
Reluctant to fly, a weather vane that traces
The flow of cloud shadow over monotonous bog –
And useless too, though it might well bring to mind
The plumpness of pillows, the staunching of wounds,

Rags torn from a petticoat and soaked in water
And tied to the bushes around some holy well
As though to make a hospital of the landscape –
Cures and medicines as far as the horizon
Which nobody harvests except with the eye.)

You saw that beyond the thirstier desert flowers
There fell hundreds of thousands of poppy petals
Magnified to blood stains by the middle distance
Or through the still unfocused sights of a rifle –
And Isaac Rosenberg wore one behind his ear.

SULPICIA

Round this particular date I have drawn a circle
For Mars, dressed myself up for him, dressed to kill:
When I let my hair down I am a sheaf of wheat
And I bring in the harvest without cutting it.

Were he to hover above me like a bird of prey
I would lay my body out, his little country,
Fields smelling of flowers, flowers in the hedgerow –
And then I would put on an overcoat of snow.

I will stumble behind him through the undergrowth
Tracking his white legs, drawing about us both
The hunters' circle: among twisted nets and snares

I will seduce him, tangle his hairs with my hairs
While the stag dashes off on one of its tangents
And boars root safely along our circumference.

GRACE DARLING

After you had steered your coble out of the storm
And left the smaller islands to break the surface,
Like draughts shaking that colossal backcloth there came
Fifty pounds from the Queen, proposals of marriage.

The daughter of a lighthouse-keeper and the saints
Who once lived there on birds' eggs, rainwater, barley
And built to keep all pilgrims at a safe distance
Circular houses with views only of the sky,

Who set timber burning on the top of a tower
Before each was launched at last in his stone coffin –
You would turn your back on mainland and suitor
To marry, then bereave the waves from Lindisfarne,

A moth against the lamp that shines still and reveals
Many small boats at sea, lifeboats, named after girls.

ON MWEELREA

I

I was lowering my body on to yours
When I put my ear to the mountain's side
And eavesdropped on water washing itself
In the locked bath-house of the underground.

When I dipped my hand among hidden sounds
It was the water's pulse at wrist and groin,
It was the water that reminded me
To leave all of my jugs and cups behind.

II

The slopes of the mountain were commonage
For me clambering over the low walls
To look for the rings of autumn mushrooms
That ripple out across the centuries.

I had made myself the worried shepherd
Of snipe twisting the grasses into curls
And tiny thatches where they hid away,
Of the sheep that grazed your maidenhair.

III

September grew to shadows on Mweelrea
Once the lambs had descended from the ridge
With their fleeces dyed, tinges of sunset,
Rowan berries, and the bracken rusting.

Behind my eyelids I could just make out
In a wash of blood and light and water
Your body colouring the mountainside
Like uncut poppies in the stubbly fields.

THE LINEN INDUSTRY

Pulling up flax after the blue flowers have fallen
And laying our handfuls in the peaty water
To rot those grasses to the bone, or building stooks
That recall the skirts of an invisible dancer,

We become a part of the linen industry
And follow its processes to the grubby town
Where fields are compacted into window-boxes
And there is little room among the big machines.

But even in our attic under the skylight
We make love on a bleach green, the whole meadow
Draped with material turning white in the sun
As though snow reluctant to melt were our attire.

What's passion but a battering of stubborn stalks,
Then a gentle combing out of fibres like hair
And a weaving of these into christening robes,
Into garments for a marriage or funeral?

Since it's like a bereavement once the labour's done
To find ourselves last workers in a dying trade,
Let flax be our matchmaker, our undertaker,
The provider of sheets for whatever the bed –

And be shy of your breasts in the presence of death,
Say that you look more beautiful in linen
Wearing white petticoats, the bow on your bodice
A butterfly attending the embroidered flowers.

SELF-PORTRAIT

My great-great-grandfather fell in top hat and tails
Across the threshold, his cigar brightly burning
While the chalk outline they had traced around his body
Got up and strolled through the door and became me,

But not before his own son had wasted a lifetime
Waiting to be made Lord Mayor of the Universe.
He was to choke to death on a difficult word
When a food particle lodged against his uvula.

I came into being alongside a twin brother
Who threatened me at first like an abortionist
Recommending suicide jumps and gin with cloves.
Then he blossomed into my guardian angel.

Peering back to the people who ploughed the Long Field
My eyes are bog holes that reflect a foreign sky.
Moustaches thatch my utterance in such a way
That no one can lipread the words from a distance.

I am, you will have noticed, all fingers and thumbs
But, then, so is the wing of a bat, a bird's wing.
I articulate through the nightingale's throat,
Sing with the vocal cords of the orang-outang.

THE WHITE BUTTERFLY

I wish that before you died
I had told you the legend,
A story from the Blaskets
About how the cabbage-white
May become the soul of one
Who lies sleeping in the fields.

Out of his mouth it wanders
And in through the eye-socket
Of an old horse's skull
To explore the corridors
And empty chamber, then
Flies back inside his lips.

This is a dream and flowers
Are bordering the journey
And the road leads on towards
That incandescent palace
Where from one room to the next
There is no one to be seen.

When I asked you as a child
How high should fences be
To keep in the butterflies,
Blood was already passing
Down median and margin
To the apex of a wing.

SEA SHANTY

I would have waited under the statue of Eros
While the wind whistled in my bell-bottoms,
Taken my bearings from the blink of daylight
Her thighs and feathery maidenhair let through.
But now from the high ground of Carrigskeewaun
I watch Lesbos rising among the islands.
Rain shivers off the machair, and exposes me
In my long-johns, who dozed on her breastbone,
On pillows of sea-pink beyond the shingle,
Who mumbled into the ringlets at her ear
My repertoire of sea shanties and love songs.
I shake like a rock-fern, and my ill will
And smoky breath seem to wither the lichens.
I am making do with what has been left me,
The saltier leaves of samphire for my salad.
At midnight the moon goes, then the Pleiades,
A sparkle of sand grains on my wellingtons.

BETWEEN HOVERS
in memory of Joe O'Toole

And not even when we ran over the badger
Did he tell me he had cancer, Joe O'Toole
Who was psychic about carburettor and clutch
And knew a folk cure for the starter-engine.
Backing into the dark we floodlit each hair
Like a filament of light our lights had put out
Somewhere between Kinnadoohy and Thallabaun.
I dragged it by two gritty paws into the ditch.
Joe spotted a ruby where the canines touched.
His way of seeing me safely across the duach
Was to leave his porch light burning, its sparkle
Shifting from widgeon to teal on Corragaun Lake.
I missed his funeral. Close to the stony roads
He lies in Killeen Churchyard over the hill.
This morning on the burial mound at Templedoomore
Encircled by a spring tide and taking in
Cloonaghmanagh and Claggan and Carrigskeewaun,
The townlands he'd wandered tending cows and sheep,
I watched a dying otter gaze right through me
At the islands in Clew Bay, as though it were only
Between hovers and not too far from the holt.

DETOUR

I want my funeral to include this detour
Down the single street of a small market town,
On either side of the procession such names
As Philbin, O'Malley, MacNamara, Keane.
A reverent pause to let a herd of milkers pass
Will bring me face to face with grubby parsnips,
Cauliflowers that glitter after a sunshower,
Then hay rakes, broom handles, gas cylinders.
Reflected in the slow sequence of shop windows
I shall be part of the action when his wife
Draining the potatoes into a steamy sink
Calls to the butcher to get ready for dinner
And the publican descends to change a barrel.
From behind the one locked door for miles around
I shall prolong a detailed conversation
With the man in the concrete telephone kiosk
About where my funeral might be going next.

REMEMBERING CARRIGSKEEWAUN

A wintry night, the hearth inhales
And the chimney becomes a windpipe
Fluffy with soot and thistledown,
A voice-box recalling animals:
The leveret come of age, snipe
At an angle, then the porpoises'
Demonstration of meaningless smiles.
Home is a hollow between the waves,
A clump of nettles, feathery winds,
And memory no longer than a day
When the animals come back to me
From the townland of Carrigskeewaun,
From a page lit by the Milky Way.

GORSE FIRES

Cattle out of their byres are dungy still, lambs
Have stepped from last year as from an enclosure.
Five or six men stand gazing at a rusty tractor
Before carrying implements to separate fields.

I am travelling from one April to another.
It is the same train between the same embankments.
Gorse fires are smoking, but primroses burn
And celandines and white may and gorse flowers.

HOMECOMING

The brightest star came out, the day-star, dawn's star
And the seafaring ship drew near to Ithaca, to home
And that harbour named after the old man of the sea, two
Headlands huddling together as breakwater, windbreak,
Haven where complicated vessels float free of moorings
In their actual mooring-places.
                              At the harbour-head
A long-leaved olive overshadows a shadowy cave
Full of bullauns, basins hollowed out of stone, stone
Jars for honey-bees, looms of stone on which are woven
Sea-purplish things – also, inextinguishable springs
And two ways in, one looking north where men descend
While the other faces south, a footpath for the gods.

When they had scrunched ashore at this familiar cove
And disembarked, they lifted Odysseus out of his hollow
Just as he was, linen sheet and glossy rug and all,
And put him to bed on the sand, still lost in sleep.

HALLEY'S COMET
Homage to Erik Satie

It was the seventeenth variation after all.
The original theme had fluttered out of my hands
And upside down on the linoleum suggested it.
An ink blot on the stave inspired the modulation,
Or was it a bloodstain, a teardrop's immortality
Perfectly pitched between parallels, horizontals,
The provisional shorelines, amphibian swamps?
I got drunk on a pint mug full of white feathers.
I couldn't sleep because inside my left nostril
A hair kept buzzing with signals from Halley's comet
As it swung its skirt of heavenly dust particles
On a parabola around the electric light bulb.
This won't recur for another seventy-six years.

AN AMISH RUG

As if a one-room schoolhouse were all we knew
And our clothes were black, our underclothes black,
Marriage a horse and buggy going to church
And the children silhouettes in a snowy field,

I bring you this patchwork like a smallholding
Where I served as the hired boy behind the harrow,
Its threads the colour of cantaloupe and cherry
Securing hay bales, corn cobs, tobacco leaves.

You may hang it on the wall, a cathedral window,
Or lay it out on the floor beside our bed
So that whenever we undress for sleep or love
We shall step over it as over a flowerbed.

TREE-HOUSE

When he described how he had built the ingenious bedroom
Around that bushy olive-tree – their sign and secret –
The stone-work tightly set, the thatching weatherproof,
Double-doors well-hinged; how he had lopped off branches
And with his adze smoothed down the trunk and got it plumb
– The beginnings of a bed, the bedpost – and with his auger
Drilled the frame, inlaying silver, ivory, gold; and then
How he had interwoven thongs of ox-hide, coloured purple –
She believed at last in the master-craftsman, Odysseus,
And tangled like a child in the imaginary branches
Of the tree-house he had built, love poet, carpenter.

COUCHETTE

With my wife, son, daughter in layers up the walls
This room on wheels has become the family vault.
They have fallen asleep, dreams stopping and starting
As my long coffin wobbles on the top couchette.
Shunted down a siding, we shall wait for centuries
Before hurtling to places we have never seen.
No more than a blink of light, a tinkle of bangles,
The old woman who joins us at Turin will leave
Crusts and a plastic bottle of mineral water.
Soon her space will be taken by a younger lady
We met four thousand years ago in Fiesole,
Her face still to be uncovered, and at her feet
A pet cat who has also been wrapped in bandages.

LAERTES

When he found Laertes alone on the tidy terrace, hoeing
Around a vine, disreputable in his gardening duds,
Patched and grubby, leather gaiters protecting his shins
Against brambles, gloves as well, and, to cap it all,
Sure sign of his deep depression, a goatskin duncher,
Odysseus sobbed in the shade of a pear-tree for his father
So old and pathetic that all he wanted then and there
Was to kiss him and hug him and blurt out the whole story,
But the whole story is one catalogue and then another,
So he waited for images from that formal garden,
Evidence of a childhood spent traipsing after his father
And asking for everything he saw, the thirteen pear-trees,
Ten apple-trees, forty fig-trees, the fifty rows of vines
Ripening at different times for a continuous supply,
Until Laertes recognised his son and, weak at the knees,
Dizzy, flung his arms around the neck of great Odysseus
Who drew the old man fainting to his breast and held him there
And cradled like driftwood the bones of his dwindling father.

ANTICLEIA

If at a rock where the resonant rivers meet, Acheron,
Pyriphlegethon, Cocytus, tributary of the Styx, you dig
A pit, about a cubit each way, from knuckles to elbow,
And sacrifice a ram and a black ewe, bending their heads
Towards the outer darkness, while you face the water,
And so many souls of the anaemic dead come crowding in
That you hold them back with your bayonet from the blood
Only to recognise among the zombies your own mother,
And if, having given her blood to drink and talked about home,
You lunge forward three times to hug her and three times
Like a shadow or idea she vanishes through your arms
And you ask her why she keeps avoiding your touch and weep
Because here is your mother and even here in Hades
You could comfort each other in a shuddering embrace,
Will she explain that the sinews no longer bind her flesh
And bones, that the irresistible fire has demolished these,
That the soul takes flight like a dream and flutters in the sky,
That this is what happens to human beings when they die?

GHETTO

I

Because you will suffer soon and die, your choices
Are neither right nor wrong: a spoon will feed you,
A flannel keep you clean, a toothbrush bring you back
To your bathroom's view of chimney-pots and gardens.
With so little time for inventory or leavetaking,
You are packing now for the rest of your life
Photographs, medicines, a change of underwear, a book,
A candlestick, a loaf, sardines, needle and thread.
These are your heirlooms, perishables, worldly goods.
What you bring is the same as what you leave behind,
Your last belonging a list of your belongings.

II

As though it were against the law to sleep on pillows
They have filled a cathedral with confiscated feathers:
Silence irrefrangible, no room for angels' wings,
Tons of feathers suffocating cherubim and seraphim.

III

The little girl without a mother behaves like a mother
With her rag doll to whom she explains fear and anguish,
The meagreness of the bread ration, how to make it last,
How to get back to the doll's house and lift up the roof
And, before the flame-throwers and dynamiters destroy it,
How to rescue from their separate rooms love and sorrow,
Masterpieces the size of a postage stamp, small fortunes.

IV

From among the hundreds of thousands I can imagine one
Behind the barbed-wire fences as my train crosses Poland.
I see him for long enough to catch the sprinkle of snowflakes
On his hair and schoolbag, and then I am transported
Away from that world of broken hobby-horses and silent toys.
He turns into a little snowman and refuses to melt.

V

For street-singers in the marketplace, weavers, warp-makers,
Those who suffer in sewing-machine repair shops, excrement-
Removal workers, there are not enough root vegetables,
Beetroots, turnips, swedes, nor for the leather-stitchers
Who are boiling leather so that their children may eat;
Who are turning like a thick slice of potato-bread
This page, which is everything I know about potatoes,
My delivery of Irish Peace, Beauty of Hebron, Home
Guard, Arran Banners, Kerr's Pinks, resistant to eelworm,
Resignation, common scab, terror, frost, potato-blight.

VI

There will be performances in the waiting room, and time
To jump over a skipping rope, and time to adjust
As though for a dancing class the ribbons in your hair.
This string quartet is the most natural thing in the world.

VII

Fingers leave shadows on a violin, harmonics,
A blackbird fluttering between electrified fences.

Lessons were forbidden in that terrible school.
Punishable by death were reading and writing
And arithmetic, so that even the junior infants
Grew old and wise in lofts studying these subjects.
There were drawing lessons, and drawings of kitchens
And farms, farm animals, butterflies, mothers, fathers
Who survived in crayon until in pen and ink
They turned into guards at executions and funerals
Torturing and hanging even these stick figures.
There were drawings of barracks and latrines as well
And the only windows were the windows they drew.

TEREZÍN

No room has ever been as silent as the room
Where hundreds of violins are hung in unison.

THE BUTCHERS

When he had made sure there were no survivors in his house
And that all the suitors were dead, heaped in blood and dust
Like fish that fishermen with fine-meshed nets have hauled
Up gasping for salt water, evaporating in the sunshine,
Odysseus, spattered with muck and like a lion dripping blood
From his chest and cheeks after devouring a farmer's bullock,
Ordered the disloyal housemaids to sponge down the armchairs
And tables, while Telemachos, the oxherd and the swineherd
Scraped the floor with shovels, and then between the portico
And the roundhouse stretched a hawser and hanged the women
So none touched the ground with her toes, like long-winged thrushes
Or doves trapped in a mist-net across the thicket where they roost,
Their heads bobbing in a row, their feet twitching but not for long,
And when they had dragged Melanthios's corpse into the haggard
And cut off his nose and ears and cock and balls, a dog's dinner,
Odysseus, seeing the need for whitewash and disinfectant,
Fumigated the house and the outhouses, so that Hermes
Like a clergyman might wave the supernatural baton
With which he resurrects or hypnotises those he chooses,
And waken and round up the suitors' souls, and the housemaids',
Like bats gibbering in the nooks of their mysterious cave
When out of the clusters that dangle from the rocky ceiling
One of them drops and squeaks, so their souls were bat-squeaks
As they flittered after Hermes, their deliverer, who led them
Along the clammy sheughs, then past the oceanic streams
And the white rock, the sun's gatepost in that dreamy region,
Until they came to a bog-meadow full of bog-asphodels
Where the residents are ghosts or images of the dead.

THE ICE-CREAM MAN

Rum and raisin, vanilla, butter-scotch, walnut, peach:
You would rhyme off the flavours. That was before
They murdered the ice-cream man on the Lisburn Road
And you bought carnations to lay outside his shop.
I named for you all the wild flowers of the Burren
I had seen in one day: thyme, valerian, loosestrife,
Meadowsweet, tway blade, crowfoot, ling, angelica,
Herb robert, marjoram, cow parsley, sundew, vetch,
Mountain avens, wood sage, ragged robin, stitchwort,
Yarrow, lady's bedstraw, bindweed, bog pimpernel.

FORM

Trying to tell it all to you and cover everything
Is like awakening from its grassy form the hare:
In that make-shift shelter your hand, then my hand
Mislays the hare and the warmth it leaves behind.

AUTUMN LADY'S TRESSES

How does the solitary swan on Dooaghtry Lake
Who knows all about the otter as a glimmer
Among reeds, as water unravelling, as watery
Corridors into the water, a sudden face,
Receive through the huge silence of sand-dunes
Signals from the otters' rock at Allaran Point
About another otter, the same otter, folding
Sunlight into the combers like brown kelp,
Or the dolphins whose waves within waves propel
You and me along the strand like young lovers,
Or the aftermath of lit thistledown, peacock
Butterflies above marram grass, lady's tresses
That wind into their spirals of white flowers
Cowrie shells for decorating your sandy hair?

When in good time corpses go off and ooze in the heat
Creepy-crawlies breed in them. Bury your prize bull
(A well-known experiment) – and from the putrid guts
Swarm flower-crazy bees, industrious country-types
Working hard, as did their host, with harvest in mind.
An interred war-horse produces hornets. Remove
A shore-crab's hollow claw, lay it to rest: the result
Is a scorpion charging with its tail bent like a hook.
Worms cosy in cocoons of white thread grow into
Butterflies, souls of the dead. Any farmer knows that.

Germs in mud generate green frogs: legless at first
They soon sprout swimming and jumping equipment.
A she-bear's cub is a lump of meat whose stumpy
Non-legs she licks into shape in her own image.
The honey-bees' larvae hatched in those waxy hexagons
Only get feet and wings later on. That's obvious.
Think of peacocks, eagles, doves, the bird-family
As a whole, all starting inside eggs: hard to believe.
There's a theory that in the grave the backbone rots
Away and the spinal cord turns into a snake.

The fundamental interconnectedness of all things
Is incredible enough, but did you know that
Hyenas change sex? The female mounted by a male
Just minutes before, becomes a male herself. Then
There's the chameleon that feeds off wind and air
And takes the colour of whatever it's standing on.
Air transforms lynxes' urine into stones and hardens
Coral, that softly swaying underwater plant.
I could go on and on with these scientific facts.
If it wasn't so late I'd tell you a whole lot more.

A FLOWERING

Now that my body grows woman-like I look at men
As two or three women have looked at me, then hide
Among Ovid's lovely casualties – all that blood
Colouring the grass and changing into flowers, purple,
Lily-shaped, wild hyacinth upon whose petals
We doodled our lugubrious initials, they and I,
Blood dosed with honey, tumescent, effervescent
– Clean bubbles in yellow mud – creating in an hour
My own son's beauty, the truthfulness of my nipples,
Petals that will not last long, that hang on and no more,
Youth and its flower named after the wind, anemone.

THE GHOST ORCHID

Added to its few remaining sites will be the stanza
I compose about leaves like flakes of skin, a colour
Dithering between pink and yellow, and then the root
That grows like coral among shadows and leaf-litter.
Just touching the petals bruises them into darkness.

THE WHITE GARDEN

So white are the white flowers in the white garden that I
Disappear in no time at all among lace and veils.
For whom do I scribble the few words that come to me
From beyond the arch of white roses as from nowhere,
My memorandum to posterity? Listen. 'The saw
Is under the garden bench and the gate is unlatched.'

A GRAIN OF RICE

Wrap my poem around your chopsticks to keep them clean.
I hardly know you. I do not want you to die. Our names
Fit on to a grain of rice like Hokusai's two sparrows,
Or else, like the praying mantis and the yellow butterfly,
We are a crowd in the garden where nothing grows but stones.
I do not understand the characters: sunlight through leaves,
An ivy pattern like fingers caressing a bowl, your face
In splinters where a carp kisses the moon, the waterfall
Up which its fins will spiral out of sight and into the sky.
Wrap my poem around your chopsticks to keep them clean.
Does it mean I shall not have taken one kiss for ever?
Your unimaginable breasts become the silkworm's shrine.

CHINESE OBJECTS

I

The length of white silk I selected
Immaculate as the crust on snow
Was cut in the shape of happiness,
Round as the moon in starry skies.
In and out of her sleeve it slides
Rustling up its own cool weather.
I worry that when autumn comes
And blows away this heatwave,
She will toss the fan into a box
Half way through our love affair.

II

When the water-gourd that dangles
Light as a single leaf from the tree
Goes clickety-clack in the breeze
So that bed-sounds and love-making
Get into my dream, in my dream
I throw it away, for the world
Is not so big, the gourd so small:
They are objects outside my body
That get in the way of sleep.

BAUCIS & PHILEMON
for Brian & Denise Ferran

In the Phrygian hills an oak tree grows beside a lime tree
And a low wall encloses them. Not far away lies bogland.
I have seen the spot myself. It should convince you
– If you need to be convinced – that the power of heaven
Is limitless, that whatever the gods desire gets done.

Where a drowned valley makes a sanctuary for water birds
(Divers, coots), a whole community used to plough – until
Jupiter brought Mercury without his wand or wings.
Disguised as humans, they knocked at a thousand houses
Looking for lodgings. A thousand houses slammed the door.

But one house took them in, a cottage thatched with straw
And reeds from the bog. Baucis and Philemon, a kindly
Old couple, had been married there when they were young
And, growing old together there, found peace of mind
By owning up to their poverty and making light of it.

Pointless to look for masters or servants here because
Wife and husband served and ruled the household equally.
So, when these sky-dwellers appeared at their cottage-home
Stooping under the low door to get in, the old man
Brought them stools to sit on, the old woman cushions.

She raked the warm ashes to one side and fanned into life
Yesterday's embers which she fed with leaves and dry bark,
The breath from her old body puffing them into flames.
She hoked around in the roof-space for twigs and firewood,
Broke them up and poked the kindling under her skillet.

She took the cabbage which Philemon had brought her
From the garden plot, and lopped off the outer leaves. He
Lowered a flitch of smoked bacon from the sooty rafters
And carved a reasonable helping from their precious pork
Which he simmered in bubbling water to make a stew.

They chatted to pass the time for their hungry visitors
And poured into a beechwood bucket dangling from its peg
Warm water so that the immortals might freshen up.
Over a sofa, its feet and frame carved out of willow,
Drooped a mattress lumpy with sedge-grass from the river.

On this they spread a coverlet, and the gods sat down.
The old woman tucked up her skirts and with shaky hands
Placed the table in front of them. Because one leg was short
She improvised a wedge and made the surface level
Before wiping it over with a sprig of water-mint.

She put on the table speckly olives and wild cherries
Pickled in wine, endives, radishes, cottage-cheese and eggs
Gently cooked in cooling ashes, all served on crockery.
Next, she produced the hand-decorated wine-jug
And beechwood cups polished inside with yellow wax.

In no time meat arrived from the fireplace piping hot
And the wine, a rough and ready vintage, went the rounds
Until they cleared the table for a second course – nuts
And figs and wrinkly dates, plums and sweet-smelling apples
In a wicker basket, purple grapes fresh from the vines.

The centrepiece was a honeycomb oozing clear honey,
And, over everything, the circle of convivial faces
And the bustle of hospitality. And then the hosts
Noticed that the wine jug, as soon as it was emptied,
Filled itself up again – an inexhaustible supply.

This looked like a miracle to Philemon and Baucis
Who, waving their hands about as if in prayer or shock,
Apologised for their home-cooking and simple recipes.
They had just one gander, guardian of the smallholding,
Whom they wanted to sacrifice for the divinities.

But he was too nippy for them and flapped out of danger
Into the immortals' arms. 'Don't kill the goose!' they thundered.
'We're gods. Your tightfisted neighbours are about to get
What they deserve. You two are granted immunity.
Abandon your home and climb the mountainside with us.'

Unsteady on their walking-sticks they struggled up the steep
Slope and glancing back, a stone's throw from the top, they saw
The townland flooded, with just their homestead high and dry.
While they stood flabbergasted, crying out for neighbours,
Their cottage (a squeeze for the two of them) became a church.

Stone pillars took the place of the home-made wooden piles,
The thatching glowed so yellow that the roof looked golden,
Filigree transformed the doorway, and marble tiling
Improved the dirt floor. Jupiter spoke like a gentleman:
'Grandpa, if you and your good wife could have one wish . . . ?'

'May we work as vergers in your chapel, and, since our lives
Have been spent together, please may we die together,
The two of us at the one time? I don't want to see
My wife buried or be buried by her.' Their wish came true
And up to the last moment they looked after the chapel.

At the end of their days when they were very old and bowed
And living on their memories, outside the chapel door
Baucis who was leafy too watched Philemon sprouting leaves.
As tree-tops overgrew their smiles they called in unison
'Goodbye, my dear'. Then the bark knitted and hid their lips.

Two trees are grafted together where their two bodies stood.
I add my flowers to bouquets in the branches by saying
'Treat those whom God loves as your local gods – a blackthorn
Or a standing stone. Take care of caretakers and watch
Over the nightwatchman and the nightwatchman's wife.'

A BED OF LEAVES

He climbed to the copse, a conspicuous place near water,
And crawled under two bushes sprouting from one stem (olive
And wild olive), a thatch so close neither gale-force winds
Nor sunlight nor cloudbursts could penetrate: it was here
Odysseus snuggled and heaped on his mattress of leaves
An eiderdown of leaves, enough to make a double-bed
In winter, whatever the weather, and smiled to himself
When he saw his bed and stretched out in the middle of it
And let even more of the fallen leaves fall over him:
As when a lonely man on a lonely farm smoors the fire
And hides a turf-sod in the ashes to save an ember,
So was his body in the bed of leaves its own kindling
And sleep settled on him like ashes and closed his eyelids.

THE OAR

I am meant to wander inland with a well-balanced oar
Until I meet people who know nothing about the sea –
Salty food, prows painted purple, oars that are ships'
Wings – and somebody mistakes the oar on my shoulder
For a winnowing fan:

                            the signal to plant it in the ground
And start saying my prayers, to go on saying my prayers
Once I'm home, weary but well looked after in old age
By my family and friends and other happy islanders,
And death will come to me, a gentle sea-breeze, no more than
An exhalation, the waft from a winnowing fan or oar.

THE CAMPFIRES

All night crackling campfires boosted their morale
As they dozed in no man's land and the killing fields.
(There are balmy nights – not a breath, constellations
Resplendent in the sky around a dazzling moon –
When a clearance high in the atmosphere unveils
The boundlessness of space, and all the stars are out
Lighting up hilltops, glens, headlands, vantage
Points like Tonakeera and Allaran where the tide
Turns into Killary, where salmon run from the sea,
Where the shepherd smiles on his luminous townland.
That many campfires sparkled in front of Ilium
Between the river and the ships, a thousand fires,
Round each one fifty men relaxing in the firelight.)
Shuffling next to the chariots, munching shiny oats
And barley, their horses waited for the sunrise.

CEASEFIRE

I

Put in mind of his own father and moved to tears
Achilles took him by the hand and pushed the old king
Gently away, but Priam curled up at his feet and
Wept with him until their sadness filled the building.

II

Taking Hector's corpse into his own hands Achilles
Made sure it was washed and, for the old king's sake,
Laid out in uniform, ready for Priam to carry
Wrapped like a present home to Troy at daybreak.

III

When they had eaten together, it pleased them both
To stare at each other's beauty as lovers might,
Achilles built like a god, Priam good-looking still
And full of conversation, who earlier had sighed:

IV

'I get down on my knees and do what must be done
And kiss Achilles' hand, the killer of my son.'

RIVER & FOUNTAIN

I

I am walking backwards into the future like a Greek.
I have nothing to say. There is nothing I would describe.
It was always thus: as if snow has fallen on Front
Square, and, feeling the downy silence of the snowflakes
That cover cobbles and each other, white erasing white,
I read shadow and snow-drift under the Campanile.

II

'It fits on to the back of a postage stamp,' Robert said
As he scribbled out in tiny symbols the equation,
His silhouette a frost-flower on the window of my last
Year, his page the sky between chimney-stacks, his head
And my head at the city's centre aching for giddy
Limits, mathematics, poetry, squeaky nibs at all hours.

III

Top of the staircase, Number Sixteen in Botany Bay,
Slum-dwellers, we survived gas-rings that popped, slop-
Buckets in the bedrooms, changeable 'wives', and toasted
Doughy doorsteps, Freshmen turning into Sophisters
In front of the higgledy flames: our still-life, crusts
And buttery books, the half-empty marmalade jar.

IV

My Dansette record player bottled up like genies
Sibelius, Shostakovich, Bruckner, dusty sleeves
Accumulating next to Liddell and Scott's *Greek-English
Lexicon* voices the fluffy needle set almost free.
I was the culture vulture from Ulster, Vincent's joke
Who heard *The Rite of Spring* and contemplated suicide.

V

Adam was first to read the maroon-covered notebooks
I filled with innocent outpourings, Adam the scholar
Whose stammer could stop him christening this and that,
Whose Eden was annotation and vocabulary lists
In a precise classicist's hand, the love of words as words.
My first and best review was Adam's 'I like these – I – I –'

VI

'College poet? Village idiot you mean!' (Vincent again).
In neither profession could I settle comfortably
Once Derek arrived reciting Rimbaud, giving names
To the constellations over the Examination Hall.
'Are you Longley? Can I borrow your typewriter? Soon?'
His was the first snow party I attended. I felt the cold.

VII

We were from the North, hitch-hikers on the Newry Road,
Faces that vanished from a hundred driving-mirrors
Down that warren of reflections – O'Neill's Bar, Nesbitt's –
And through Front Gate to Connemara and Inishere,
The raw experience of market towns and clachans, then
Back to Rooms, village of minds, poetry's townland.

VIII

Though College Square in Belfast and the Linen Hall
Had been our patch, nobody mentioned William Drennan.
In Dublin what dreams of liberty, the Index, the Ban:
Etonians on Commons cut our accents with a knife.
When Brendan from Ballylongford defied the Bishop, we
Flapped our wings together and were melted in the sun.

IX

A bath-house lotus-eater – fags, sodden *Irish Times* –
I tagged along with the Fabians, to embarrass Church
And State our grand design. Would-be class-warriors
We raised, for a moment, the Red Flag at the Rubrics,
Then joined the Civil Service and talked of Civil Rights.
Was Trinity a Trojan Horse? Were we Greeks at all?

X

'The Golden Mean is a tension, Ladies, Gentlemen,
And not a dead level': the Homeric head of Stanford
Who would nearly sing the first lines of the *Odyssey*.
That year I should have failed, but, teaching the *Poetics*,
He asked us for definitions, and accepted mine:
'Sir, if prose is a river, then poetry's a fountain.'

XI

Someone has skipped the seminar. Imagine his face,
The children's faces, my wife's: she sat beside me then
And they were waiting to be born, ghosts from a future
Without Tom: he fell in love just once and died of it.
Oh, to have turned away from everything to one face,
Eros and Thanatos your gods, icicle and dew.

XII

Walking forwards into the past with more of an idea
I want to say to my friends of thirty years ago
And to daughters and a son that Belfast is our home,
Prose a river still – the Liffey, the Lagan – and poetry
A fountain that plays in an imaginary Front Square.
When snow falls it is feathers from the wings of Icarus.

THE WEATHER IN JAPAN

Makes bead curtains of the rain,
Of the mist a paper screen.

THE COMBER

A moment before the comber turns into
A breaker – sea-spray, raggedy rainbows –
Water and sunlight contain all the colours
And suspend between Inishbofin and me
The otter, and thus we meet, without my scent
In her nostrils, the uproar of my presence,
My unforgivable shadow on the sand –
Even if this is the only sound I make.

ALL OF THESE PEOPLE

Who was it who suggested that the opposite of war
Is not so much peace as civilisation? He knew
Our assassinated Catholic greengrocer who died
At Christmas in the arms of our Methodist minister,
And our ice-cream man whose continuing requiem
Is the twenty-one flavours children have by heart.
Our cobbler mends shoes for everybody; our butcher
Blends into his best sausages leeks, garlic, honey;
Our cornershop sells everything from bread to kindling.
Who can bring peace to people who are not civilised?
All of these people, alive or dead, are civilised.

AT POLL SALACH
Easter Sunday, 1998

While I was looking for Easter snow on the hills
You showed me, like a concentration of violets
Or a fragment from some future unimagined sky,
A single spring gentian shivering at our feet.

A POPPY

When millions march into the mincing machine
An image in Homer picks out the individual
Tommy and the doughboy in his doughboy helmet:
'Lolling to one side like a poppy in a garden
Weighed down by its seed capsule and rainwater,
His head drooped under the heavy, crestfallen
Helmet' (an image Virgil steals – *lasso papavera*
Collo – and so do I), and so Gorgythion dies,
And the poppy that sheds its flower-heads in a day
Grows in one summer four hundred more, which means
Two thousand petals overlapping as though to make
A cape for the corn goddess or a soldier's soul.

POETRY

When he was billeted in a ruined house in Arras
And found a hole in the wall beside his bed
And, rummaging inside, his hand rested on *Keats*
By Edward Thomas, did Edmund Blunden unearth
A volume which 'the tall, Shelley-like figure'
Gathering up for the last time his latherbrush,
Razor, towel, comb, cardigan, cap comforter,
Water bottle, socks, gas mask, great coat, rifle
And bayonet, hurrying out of the same building
To join his men and march into battle, left
Behind him like a gift, the author's own copy?
When Thomas Hardy died his widow gave Blunden
As a memento of many visits to Max Gate
His treasured copy of Edward Thomas's *Poems*.

THE WAR GRAVES

The exhausted cathedral reaches nowhere near the sky
As though behind its buttresses wounded angels
Snooze in a halfway house of gargoyles, rainwater
By the mouthful, broken wings among pigeons' wings.

There will be no end to clearing up after the war
And only an imaginary harvest-home where once
The Germans drilled holes for dynamite, for fieldmice
To smuggle seeds and sow them inside these columns.

The headstones wipe out the horizon like a blizzard
And we can see no farther than the day they died,
As though all of them died together on the same day
And the war was that single momentous explosion.

Mothers and widows pruned these roses yesterday,
It seems, planted sweet william and mowed the lawn
After consultations with the dead, heads meeting
Over this year's seed catalogues and packets of seeds.

Around the shell holes not one poppy has appeared,
No symbolic flora, only the tiny whitish flowers
No one remembers the names of in time, brookweed
And fairy flax, say, lamb's lettuce and penny-cress.

In mine craters so vast they are called after cities
Violets thrive, as though strewn by each cataclysm
To sweeten the atmosphere and conceal death's smell
With a perfume that vanishes as soon as it is found.

At the Canadian front line permanent sandbags
And duckboards admit us to the underworld, and then
With the beavers we surface for long enough to hear
The huge lamentations of the wounded caribou.

Old pals in the visitors' book at Railway Hollow
Have scribbled 'The severest spot. The lads did well'
'We came to remember', and the woodpigeons too
Call from the wood and all the way from Accrington.

I don't know how Rifleman Parfitt, Corporal Vance,
Private Costello of the Duke of Wellingtons,
Driver Chapman, Topping, Atkinson, Duckworth,
Dorrell, Wood come to be written in my diary.

For as high as we can reach we touch-read the names
Of the disappeared, and shut our eyes and listen to
Finches' chitters and a blackbird's apprehensive cry
Accompanying Charles Sorley's monumental sonnet.

We describe the comet at Edward Thomas's grave
And, because he was a fisherman, that headlong
Motionless deflection looks like a fisherman's fly,
Two or three white after-feathers overlapping.

Geese on sentry duty, lambs, a clattering freight train
And a village graveyard encompass Wilfred Owen's
Allotment, and there we pick from a nettle bed
One celandine each, the flower that outwits winter.

THE EVENING STAR
in memory of Catherine Mercer, 1994–96

The day we buried your two years and two months
So many crocuses and snowdrops came out for you
I tried to isolate from those galaxies one flower:
A snowdrop appeared in the sky at dayligone,

The evening star, the star in Sappho's epigram
Which brings back everything that shiny daybreak
Scatters, which brings the sheep and brings the goat
And brings the wean back home to her mammy.

THE HORSES

For all of the horses butchered on the battlefield,
Shell-shocked, tripping up over their own intestines,
Drowning in the mud, the best war memorial
Is in Homer: two horses that refuse to budge
Despite threats and sweet-talk and the whistling whip,
Immovable as a tombstone, their heads drooping
In front of the streamlined motionless chariot,
Hot tears spilling from their eyelids onto the ground
Because they are still in mourning for Patroclus
Their charioteer, their shiny manes bedraggled
Under the yoke pads on either side of the yoke.

OCEAN
Homage to James 'Mick' Magennis VC

At the performance of Merce Cunningham's *Ocean*
In the Waterfront Hall the coral-coloured dancers
Drenched my head with silence and whale messages
And made me feel like a frogman on dry land.

There was room for only one midget submarine
In the roof space where my mind had floated, and where
Swimming from the Falls Road Baths to Singapore
Mick Magennis emerged in his frogman's suit,

Oxygen leaking in telltale bubbles up to heaven,
His expression unfathomable behind the visor
But his modest thumbs-up confirming that, yes,
He had stuck limpet mines on the cruiser *Takao*.

Alongside dog-paddling, ballet-dancing polar bears,
Penguins like torpedoes, dolphins in twos and threes,
Sea otters, seals, Mick was formation-swimming and
At home in the ocean's cupola above my head.

A LINEN HANDKERCHIEF
for Helen Lewis

Northern Bohemia's flax fields and the flax fields
Of Northern Ireland, the linen industry, brought Harry,
Trader in linen handkerchiefs, to Belfast, and then
After Terezín and widowhood and Auschwitz, you,

Odysseus as a girl, your sail a linen handkerchief
On which he embroidered and unpicked hundreds of names
All through the war, but in one corner the flowers
Encircling your initials never came undone.

THE DESIGN

Sometimes the quilts were white for weddings, the design
Made up of stitches and the shadows cast by stitches.
And the quilts for funerals? How do you sew the night?

THE ALTAR CLOTH
in memory of Marie Ewart

I

You poked your knitting needles through the ball of wool
And laid them beside your glasses on an open book.
You gave the fish in your fish soup a German name.
To begin with you seemed small and elderly to me.

Then you expanded and grew young and beautiful,
Your laughter a wild duck's navigational call,
Your argumentativeness Alexandrian, obstreperous
Your liking for big obstreperous dogs with big tails.

Wherever you are I would have in your vicinity
Wild figs ripening along the bumpiest side-road
And, even if an adder dozes near that carpet,
Masses of cyclamens on the path to the waterfall.

II

In the Piazza Vecchia there are only two houses,
Yours and San Rocco's chapel, so diminutive
It fits like a kennel the saint and the faithful dog
That brings him a loaf of bread daily in the story.

The falling star we saw the night before his festival
May have had nothing to do with his birthmark
Shaped like a cross, or the plague sore on his thigh
He keeps lifting the hem of his tunic to show us,

But, for the split second it managed to stay alight,
The meteor was heading for your household and his
Which is furnished with one table, candlesticks
And shell cases from the last war filled with flowers.

III

Think of San Giorgio's church who takes the dragon on
And leaves hardly any room for the undersized saint
Balancing the altar on his head, custodian,
We agree, of all we love about the Romanesque.

Shouldn't we be sheltering beneath the altar cloth's
Pattern of grapes and vine leaves, for this is our last
Conversation and the crab is nipping your synapses,
Sifting your memory through its claws and frilly lips?

Marie, I only know this in retrospect. Otherwise
I'd have washed your hair and tranquillised your brain
With evening mist that fills the Valle del Serchio and
Lingers at the bottom of the village between the vines.

THE RABBIT
for Ciaran Carson

I closed my eyes on a white horse pulling a plough
In Poland, on a haystack built around a pole,
And opened them when the young girl and her lover
Took out of a perforated cardboard shoe-box
A grey rabbit, an agreeable shitty smell,
Turds like a broken rosary, the slow train
Rocking this dainty manger scene, so that I
With a priestly forefinger tried to tickle
The narrow brain-space behind dewdrop eyes
And it bounced from her lap and from her shoulder
Kept mouthing 'prunes and prisms' as if to warn
That even with so little to say for itself
A silly rabbit could pick up like a scent trail
My gynaecological concept of the warren
With its entrances and innermost chamber,
Or the heroic survival in Warsaw's sewers
Of just one bunny saved as a pet or meal,
Or its afterlife as *Hasenpfeffer* with cloves
And bay leaves, onions – enough! – and so
It would make its getaway when next I dozed
Crossing the Oder, somewhere in Silesia
(Silesian lettuce, h'm), never to meet again,
Or so I thought, until in Lodz in the small hours
A fat hilarious prostitute let that rabbit bop
Across her shoulders without tousling her hair-do
And burrow under her chin and nuzzle her ear
As though it were crooning 'The Groves of Blarney'
Or 'She Walked Unaware', then in her cleavage
It crouched as in a ploughed furrow, ears laid flat,
Pretending to be a stone, safe from stoat and fox.

ETRURIA

Pavese's English poems, an English setter barking –
Too hot and clammy to read, sleep, dander, so
Snap my walking stick in two and lay it out beside
My long bones in an ossuary that tells a story,

The apprentice ivory carver's yarn, for instance,
Who etched those elderly twinkling Chinese pilgrims
On a walnut, shell-crinkles their only obstacle,
Globe-trotters in my palm, the kernel still rattling.

You can find me under the sellotaped map fold
Stuck with dog hairs, and close to a mulberry bush
The women tended, coddling between their breasts
The silkworms' filaments, vulnerable bobbins.

Was it a humming bird or a humming bird moth
Mistook my navel for some chubby convolvulus?
Paolo steps from his *casa* like an astronaut
And stoops with smoky bellows among his bees.

Gin, acacia honey, last year's sloes, crimson
Slipping its gravity like the satellite that swims
In and out of the hanging hornet-traps, then
Jukes between midnight planes and shooting stars.

The trout that dozed in a perfect circle wear
Prison grey in the fridge, bellies sky-coloured
Next to the butter dish's pattern, traveller's joy,
Old man's beard when it seeds, feathery plumes.

The melon Adua leaves me on the windowsill
Gift-wrapped in a paper bag and moonlight,
Ripens in moon-breezes, the pipistrelle's whooshes,
My own breathing and the insomniac aspen's.

A liver concocted out of darkness and wine
Dregs, the vinegar mother sulking in her crock
Haruspicates fever, shrivelled grapes, vipers
On the footpath to a non-existent waterfall.

I escape the amorous mongrel with dewclaws
And vanish where once the privy stood, my kaftan
Snagging on the spiral staircase down to the small
Hours when house and I get into bed together,

My mattress on the floor, crickets, scorpion shapes
In their moonlit square, my space in this cellar
Beneath old rafters and old stones, Etruria,
Nightmare's cesspit, the mosquito-buzz of sleep.

THE WATERFALL

If you were to read my poems, all of them, I mean,
My life's work, at the one sitting, in the one place,
Let it be here by this half-hearted waterfall
That allows each pebbly basin its separate say,
Damp stones and syllables, then, as it grows dark
And you go home past overgrown vineyards and
Chestnut trees, suppliers once of crossbeams, moon-
Shaped nuts, flour, and crackly stuffing for mattresses,
Leave them here, on the page, in your mind's eye, lit
Like the fireflies at the waterfall, a wall of stars.

THE BEECH TREE

Leaning back like a lover against this beech tree's
Two-hundred-year-old pewter trunk, I look up
Through skylights into the leafy cumulus, and join
Everybody who has teetered where these huge roots
Spread far and wide our motionless mossy dance,
As though I'd begun my eclogues with a beech
As Virgil does, the brown envelopes unfolding
Like fans their transparent downy leaves, tassels
And prickly cups, mast, a fall of vermilion
And copper and gold, then room in the branches
For the full moon and her dusty lakes, winter
And the poet who recollects his younger self
And improvises a last line for the georgics
About snoozing under this beech tree's canopy.

REMEMBERING THE POETS

As a teenage poet I idolised the poets, doddery
Macer trying out his *Ornithogonia* on me,
And the other one about herbal cures for snake bites,
Propertius, my soul mate, love's polysyllabic
Pyrotechnical laureate reciting reams by heart,
Ponticus straining to write The Long Poem, Bassus
(Sorry for dropping names) iambic to a fault,
Horace hypnotising me with songs on the guitar,
Virgil, our homespun internationalist, sighted
At some government reception, and then Albius
Tibullus strolling in the woods a little while
With me before he died, his two slim volumes
An echo from the past, a melodious complaint
That reaches me here, the last of the singing line.

BIRDS & FLOWERS
for Fuyuji Tanigawa

My local The Chelsea where I took you for a pint
Has been demolished, which leaves us drinking in the rain,
Two inky smiles on handkerchiefs tied for luck like dolls
Flapping where the window should be, in Ireland or Japan.

A wagtail pauses among maple leaves turning from red
To pink in the picture you enclose with your good news:
'I have been a man of home these years,' you write, 'often
Surprised to know so much passion hidden in myself.'

You who translated for me 'ichigo-ichie' as 'one life,
One meeting' as though each encounter were once-in-a-
Lifetime, have been spending time with your little children:
'But I will go back to the world of letters soon.' Fuyuji,

The world of letters is a treacherous place. We are weak
And unstable. Let us float naked again in volcanic
Pools under the constellations and talk about babies.
The picture you sent to Belfast is called 'Birds & Flowers'.

SNOW WATER

A fastidious brewer of tea, a tea
Connoisseur as well as a poet,
I modestly request on my sixtieth
Birthday a gift of snow water.

Tea steam and ink stains. Single-
Mindedly I scald my teapot and
Measure out some Silver Needles Tea,
Enough for a second steeping.

Other favourites include Clear
Distance and Eyebrows of Longevity
Or, from precarious mountain peaks,
Cloud Mist Tea (quite delectable)

Which competent monkeys harvest
Filling their baskets with choice leaves
And bringing them down to where I wait
With my crock of snow water.

ABOVE DOOAGHTRY

Where the duach rises to a small plateau
That overlooks the sand dunes from Dooaghtry
To Roonkeel, and just beyond the cottage's
Higgledy perimeter fence-posts
At Carrigskeewaun, bury my ashes,

For the burial mound at Templedoomore
Has been erased by wind and sea, the same
Old stone-age sea that came as far inland
As Cloonaghmanagh and chose the place
That I choose as a promontory, a fort:

Let boulders at the top encircle me,
Neither a drystone wall nor a cairn, space
For the otter to die and the mountain hare
To lick snow stains from her underside,
A table for the peregrine and ravens,

A prickly double-bed as well, nettles
And carline-thistles, a sheeps' wool pillow,
So that, should she decide to join me there,
Our sandy dander to Allaran Point
Or Tonakeera will take for ever.

PETALWORT
for Michael Viney

You want your ashes to swirl along the strand
At Thallabaun – amongst clockwork, approachable,
Circumambulatory sanderlings, crab shells,
Bladderwrack, phosphorescence at spring tide –

Around the burial mound's wind-and-wave-inspired
Vanishing act – through dowel-holes in the wreck –
Into bottles but without a message, only
Self-effacement in sand, additional eddies.

There's no such place as heaven, so let it be
The Carricknashinnagh shoal or Caher
Island where you honeymooned in a tent
Amid the pilgrim-fishermen's stations,

Your spillet disentangling and trailing off
Into the night, a ghost on every hook – dab
And flounder, thorny skate – at ebb tide you
Kneeling on watery sand to haul them in.

Let us choose for the wreath a flower so small
Even you haven't spotted on the dune-slack
Between Claggan and Lackakeely its rosette –
Petalwort: snail snack, angel's nosegay.

CEILIDH

A ceilidh at Carrigskeewaun would now include
The ghost of Joe O'Toole at ease on his hummock
The far side of Corragaun Lake as he listens to
The O'Tooles from Inishdeigil who settled here
Eighty years ago, thirteen O'Tooles, each of them
A singer or fiddler, thirteen under the one roof,
A happy family but an unlucky one, Joe says,
And the visitors from Connemara who have rowed
Their currachs across the Killary for the music,
And my ghost at the duach's sheepbitten edge
Keeping an eye on the lamps in the windows here
But distracted by the nervy plover that pretends
A broken wing, by the long-lived oystercatcher
That calls out behind me from Thallabaun Strand.
The thirteen O'Tooles are singing about everything.
Their salty eggs are cherished for miles around.
There's a hazel copse near the lake without a name.
Dog violets, sorrel, wood spurge are growing there.
On Inishdeigil there's a well of the purest water.
Is that Arcturus or a faraway outhouse light?
The crescent moon's a coracle for Venus. Look.
Through the tide and over the Owenadornaun
Are shouldered the coffins of the thirteen O'Tooles.

THE PATTERN

Thirty-six years, to the day, after our wedding
When a cold figure-revealing wind blew against you
And lifted your veil, I find in its fat envelope
The six-shilling *Vogue* pattern for your bride's dress,
Complicated instructions for stitching bodice
And skirt, box pleats and hems, tissue-paper outlines,
Semblances of skin which I nervously unfold
And hold up in snow light, for snow has been falling
On this windless day, and I glimpse your wedding dress
And white shoes outside in the transformed garden
Where the clothesline and every twig have been covered.

STONECHAT

A flicker on the highest twig, a breast
That kindles the last of the fuchsia flowers
And the October sunset still to come
When we face the Carricknashinnagh shoal
And all the islands in a golden backwash
Where sanderlings scurry, two cormorants
Peeking at me and you over breakers
That interrupt the glow, behind us
A rainbow ascending out of Roonkeel
High above Six Noggins, disappearing
Between Mweelrea's crests, and we return
To the white cottage with its fuchsia hedge
To share for a second time the stonechat's
Flirtatious tail and flinty scolding.

ROBIN

A robin is singing from the cottage chimney.
Departure means stepping through the sound-drapes
Of his pessimistic skin-and-bone aubade.
Household chores begin: wiping wet windows
For Venus in greeny solitariness, sky-coin,
Morning's retina; scattering from the wonky
Bucket immaterial ashes over moor grass
Turned suddenly redder at the equinox;
Spreading newspapers by the hearth for blackened
Hailstones. We have slept next to the whoopers'
Nightlong echoing domestic hubbub.
A watery sun-glare is melting them.
His shadow on the lawn betrays the robin.
I would count the swans but it hurts my eyes.

PRIMARY COLOURS

When Sarah went out painting in the wind,
A gust blew the palette from her hand
And splattered with primary colours
The footprints of wild animals.

She carried home *Low Cloud on Mweelrea*
And *Storm over Lackakeely*, leaving
Burnt Umber behind for the mountain hare
And for the otter Ultramarine.

OWL CASES
for Medbh McGuckian

Leaving breath-haze and fingerprints
All over the glass case that contains
Barn-and-steeple familiars, we
Pick out the owl that is all ears,
As though tuning in with its feathers
To the togetherness of our heads.

Let us absorb Bubo bubo's
Hare-splitting claws, and such dark eyes
Above that wavering hoot (you know
The one) which is the voice of God,
And the face shaped like a heart
Or the shriek from a hollow tree.

We overlook the snowy owl
Snowdrifting in its separate case
Where it hunts by day, whose yellow gaze
Follows around the museum
Me and you, my dear, owl-lovers,
Lovers of otherworldliness.

COUPLET

When all the reeds are swaying in the wind
How can you tell which reeds the otters bend?

LEVEL PEGGING
for Michael Allen

I

After a whole day shore fishing off Allaran Point
And Tonakeera you brought back one mackerel
Which I cooked with reverence and mustard sauce.
At the stepping stones near the burial mound
I tickled a somnolent salmon to death for you.
We nabbed nothing at all with the butterfly net.

Hunters, gatherers, would-be retiarii
We succeeded at least in entangling ourselves.
When the red Canadian kite became invisible
In Donegal, we fastened the line to a bollard
And sat for hours and looked at people on the pier
Looking up at our sky-dot, fishing in the sky.

II

You were driving my Escort in the Mournes when –
Brake-failure – Robert Lowell and you careered
Downhill: 'Longley's car is a bundle of wounds.'
When his last big poem had done for Hugh MacDiarmid
And he collapsed, we wrapped his dentures in a hanky
And carried them like a relic to the hospital.

We looked after poets after a fashion. And you
Who over the decades in the Crown, the Eglantine,
The Bot, the Wellie, the Chelsea have washed down
Poetry and pottage without splashing a page
And scanned for life-threatening affectation
My latest 'wee poem' – you have looked after me.

III

I was a booby-trapped corpse in the squaddies' sights.
The arsehole of nowhere. Dawn in a mountainy bog.
From the back seat alcohol fumed as I slumbered
Surrounded by Paras, then – all innocence – you
Turned up with explanations and a petrol can.
They lowered their rifles when I opened my eyes.

Our Stingers-and-Harvey-Wallbangers period
With its plaintive anthem 'The Long and Winding Road'
Was a time of assassinations, tit-for-tat
Terror. You were Ulster's only floating voter, your
Political intelligence a wonky hedgehopping
Bi-plane that looped the loop above the killing fields.

IV

Rubbed out by winds Anaximenes imagined,
The burial mound at Templedoomore has gone.
Locals have driven their tractors along the strand
And tugged apart the wooden wreck for gateposts.
There are fewer exits than you'd think, fewer spars
For us to build our ship of death and sail away.

Remember playing cards to the crash of breakers,
Snipe drumming from the estuary, smoky gossip
In Carrigskeewaun about marriages and making wills?
I'll cut if you deal – a last game of cribbage, burnt
Matches our representatives, stick men who race
Slowly round the board with peg legs stuck in the hole.

EDWARD THOMAS'S POEM

I

I couldn't make out the minuscule handwriting
In the notebook the size of his palm and crinkled
Like an origami quim by shell-blast that stopped
His pocket watch at death. I couldn't read the poem.

II

From where he lay he could hear the skylark's
Skyward exultation, a chaffinch to his left
Fidgeting among the fallen branches,
Then all the birds of the Western Front.

III

The nature poet turned into a war poet as if
He could cure death with the rub of a dock leaf.

HARMONICA

A Tommy drops his harmonica in No Man's Land.
My dad like old Anaximenes breathes in and out
Through the holes and reeds and finds this melody.

Our souls are air. They hold us together. Listen.
A music-hall favourite lasts until the end of time.
My dad is playing it. His breath contains the world.

The wind is playing an orchestra of harmonicas.

SLEEP & DEATH

Zeus the cloud-gatherer said to sunny Apollo:
'Sponge the congealed blood from Sarpedon's corpse,
Take him far away from here, out of the line of fire,
Wash him properly in a stream, in running water,
And rub supernatural preservative over him
And wrap him up in imperishable fabrics,
Then hand him over to those speedy chaperons,
Sleep and his twin brother Death, who will bring him
In no time at all to Lycia's abundant farmland
Where his family will bury him with grave-mound
And grave-stone, the entitlement of the dead.'
And Apollo did exactly as he was told:
He carried Sarpedon out of the line of fire,
Washed him properly in a stream, in running water,
And rubbed supernatural preservative over him
And wrapped him up in imperishable fabrics
And handed him over to the speedy chaperons,
Sleep and his twin brother Death, who brought him
In no time at all to Lycia's abundant farmland.

HERON
in memory of Kenneth Koch

You died the day I was driving to Carrigskeewaun
(A remote townland in County Mayo, I explain,
Meaning, so far as I know, The Rock of the Wall Fern)
And although it was the wettest Irish year I got the car
Across the river and through the tide with groceries
And laundry for my fortnight among the waterbirds.
If I'd known you were dying, Kenneth, I'd have packed
Into cardboard boxes all your plays and poems as well
And added to curlew and lapwing anxiety-calls
The lyric intensity of your New York Jewish laughter.
You would have loved the sandy drive over the duach
('The what?'), over the machair ('the what?'), the drive
Through the white gateposts and the galvanised gate
Tied with red string, the starlings' sleeping quarters,
The drive towards turf-fired hilarity and disbelief,
'Where are all those otters, Longley, and all those hares?
I see only sparrows here and house sparrows at that!'
You are so tall and skinny I shall conscript a heron
To watch over you on hang-glider wings, old soldier,
An ashy heron, *ardea cinerea,* I remind you
(A pedant neither smallminded nor halfhearted):
'And *cinerarius*?': a slave who heats the iron tongs
In hot ashes for the hair-dresser, a hair-curler
Who will look after every hair on your curly head.
That afternoon was your night-season. I didn't know.
I didn't know that you were 'poured out like water
And all your bones were out of joint'. I didn't know.
Tuck your head in like a heron and trail behind you
Your long legs, take to the air above a townland
That encloses Carrigskeewaun and Central Park.

HELEN'S MONKEY

You saw the exhaust and inlet ports as ears,
The hole for measuring Top Dead Centre
(Piston-timing) as a nose, making the eyes
Valve-inspection covers (no longer there).
It took time, Helen, for the monkey's skull
(The cylinder head from a twenties Blackburne)
To find a body: it sat on the windowsill
Through a long evolutionary autumn
Until you came across the unimaginable –
The frame of a motorbike (and a side-car's)
Hidden by snow and heather up a hill
Near Ullapool, a twenties Blackburne of course,
Skeleton recognising skull, and soul
A monkey's soul amalgamated with yours.

PRAXILLA

Sunlight strews leaf-shadows on the kitchen floor.
Is it the beech tree or the basil plant or both?
Praxilla was *not* 'feeble-minded' to have Adonis
Answer that questionnaire in the underworld:
'Sunlight's the most beautiful thing I leave behind,
Then the shimmering stars and the moon's face,
Also ripe cucumbers and apples and pears.'
She is helping me unpack these plastic bags.
I subsist on fragments and improvisations.
Lysippus made a bronze statue of Praxilla
Who 'said nothing worthwhile in her poetry'
And set her groceries alongside the sun and moon.

THE LEVERET
for my grandson, Benjamin

This is your first night in Carrigskeewaun.
The Owennadornaun is so full of rain
You arrived in Paddy Morrison's tractor,
A bumpy approach in your father's arms
To the cottage where, all of one year ago,
You were conceived, a fire-seed in the hearth.
Did you hear the wind in the fluffy chimney?
Do you hear the wind tonight, and the rain
And a shore bird calling from the mussel reefs?
Tomorrow I'll introduce you to the sea,
Little hoplite. Have you been missing it?
I'll park your chariot by the otters' rock
And carry you over seaweed to the sea.
There's a tufted duck on David's lake
With her sootfall of hatchlings, pompoms
A day old and already learning to dive.
We may meet the stoat near the erratic
Boulder, a shrew in his mouth, or the merlin
Meadow-pipit-hunting. But don't be afraid.
The leveret breakfasts under the fuchsia
Every morning, and we shall be watching.
I have picked wild flowers for you, scabious
And centaury in a jam-jar of water
That will bend and magnify the daylight.
This is your first night in Carrigskeewaun.

THE WREN

I am writing too much about Carrigskeewaun,
I think, until you two come along, my grandsons,
And we generalise at once about cows and sheep.
A day here represents a life-time, bird's-foot trefoil
Among wild thyme, dawn and dusk muddled on the ground,
The crescent moon fading above Mweelrea's shoulder
As hares sip brackish water at the stepping stones
And the innovative raven flips upside down
As though for you.
                              I burble under your siesta
Like a contrapuntal runnel, and the heather
Stand that shelters the lesser twayblade shelters you.
We sleepwalk around a townland whooper swans
From the tundra remember, and the Saharan
Wheatear. I want you both to remember me
And what the wind-tousled wren has been saying
All day long from fence posts and the fuchsia depths,
A brain-rattling bramble-song inside a knothole.

BEE ORCHID

We returned to the Byzantine path's
Camomile-strewn marble pavement
And dusty oregano to look again,
Before the snails, for the bee orchid.

Pollinium like a brain, the brainy
Bumble-bee disguise. On our knees
Among wild garlic, almost at prayer,
We forgot about adder and lizard,

And nearly missed in a juniper
The blackcap's jet black. We waited
And waited for his connoisseur's
Restrained aria among the prickles.

CLOUDBERRIES

You give me cloudberry jam from Lapland,
Bog amber, snow-line titbits, scrumptious
Cloudberries sweetened slowly by the cold,
And costly enough for cloudberry wars
(Diplomatic wars, my dear).
                              Imagine us
Among the harvesters, keeping our distance
In sphagnum fields on the longest day
When dawn and dusk like frustrated lovers
Can kiss, legend has it, once a year. Ah,
Kisses at our age, cloudberry kisses.

GARDENING IN CARDOSO

Wild flowers become weeds
In this small triangular
Garfagnana garden
Where I uproot herb robert,
Spurge, wall-devouring
Valerian, garlicky
Ramsons, dead nettles.
What about oregano
No higher than dogs' piss,
And pennywort protecting
The lizard's hideaway?
I cut back the wild fig tree,
Its roots under the *casa*
Squeezing our waterpipes,
Dozy snails its only fruit.
From acacia – beeless,
Unrelieved – a sexual
Heaviness marries me
And five old women – last
In the village to chant
The Whitsun rosary next
Door at San Rocco's shrine.
I leave them shepherd's purse's
Seed pods – little hearts –
Spoon-shaped petals on spikes.

THE LIFEBOAT

I have imagined an ideal death in Charlie Gaffney's
Pub in Louisburgh: he pulls me the pluperfect pint
As I, at the end of the bar next the charity boxes,
Expire on my stool, head in hand, without a murmur.

I have just helped him to solve his crossword puzzle
And we commune with ancestral photos in the alcove.
He doesn't notice that I am dead until closing time
And he sweeps around my feet.
                      But it's Charlie Gaffney
Who has died. Charlie, how do I buy a fishing licence?
Shall I let the dog out? Would the fire take another sod?
The pub might as well be empty forever now. I launch
The toy lifeboat at my elbow with an old penny.

CITATION

It is like a poem. It is better than a poem,
The citation for my father's Military Cross
Dividing itself up into lines like this: 'For
Conspicuous gallantry and devotion to duty
In leading the waves of his company in a raid
And being the first to enter both objectives
In spite of a severe shrapnel wound in the thigh.
After killing several of the enemy himself,
He directed the fire of his Lewis gunners
And rifle bombers on to a working party
Of over 100 of the enemy, and controlled
The mopping-up of the enemy dug-outs.'
Kept alive by his war cry and momentum,
I shiver behind him on the fire-step.

ALTARPIECE

The page-boy in the bottom right-hand corner
Looks out and draws me into the diagonal
Drama. Or so I thought. Rather, he brings
Histrionic saint and successful soldier
(A Titian self-portrait?) down to my level.

I'm distracted already by the German bomb
Displayed on the wall next to the painting.
It pierced in February nineteen-eighteen
The basilica roof but failed to explode,
A girl's breast falling still, a rusty teardrop.

The page-boy catches my eye before I go.
Buskers are serenading Mother and Child.
We need more angels, cloud-treaders, cherubic
Instrumentalists, bomb-disposal experts.
The sky is a minefield. We shall all get hurt.

CLOUD ORCHID
in memory of Raymond Piper

Ours was a language of flowers,
As Christopher Smart would have it:
An Antrim meadow, unimproved,
Covered in lady's smock and ragged
Robin; pink pyramids at Killard;
The colours of the Union Flag
In the Republic – gentian,
Avens, cranesbill – our Ulster joke;
Spring gentian's ultimate blue
The secret of the cosmos, close
To the ground among the grasses.

You are standing and pointing, first
At the cheeky Sheila-na-gig,
Then at her offspring – unexpected
Bee orchids – around her doorway
In Kilnaboy; near Lough Bunny
Like an antique flasher in the wind
Spreading your overcoat to screen
A frantic dropwort; after
Our solitary fly orchid,
Conjuring on a bridge for me
Clouds of orange-tipped butterflies.

Undistracted in your greenhouse-
Studio by caterpillar
Droppings from the mimosa tree
That twisted overhead, you
Gazed up through the branches and
The broken pane imagining
Your last flower portrait – 'for flowers
Are good both for the living
And the dead' – the minuscule
Cloud Orchid that grows in the rain
Forest's misty canopy.

The rusty fuse you brought home
From a specific hummock
In Carrigskeewaun – autumn
Lady's-tresses – yet to flower
Under your greenhouse's moony
Glass in Belfast – do you want
Me to move it from the sill
Onto the ground for moisture
Or re-pot it or hire, as once
We did, *Mystical Rose*
And chug out to the Saltees?

WHITE FARMHOUSE

Colin Middleton knew that he was dying
And fitted all the colours he had ever used
Into his last painting, a white farmhouse
Among drumlins, the gable and chimneys
White, the corn harvested by his palette-knife,
A besmirching of corn poppy, cornflower,
One blue-black spinney, triangles of sunlight
Disappearing between Octobery hedges,
Another farmhouse in the distance like home.
Colin Middleton was a friend of mine
When I was young. How can I count the colours?
There are no doors or windows in the building,
No outhouses. I name the picture for myself.
Titles, said Duchamp, are invisible colours.

THE STAIRWELL
for Lucy McDiarmid

I have been thinking about the music for my funeral –
Liszt's transcription of that Schumann song, for instance,
'Dedication' – inwardness meets the poetry of excess –
When you lead me out of your apartment to demonstrate
In the Halloween-decorated lobby the perfect acoustic
Of the stairwell, and stand among pumpkins, cobwebby
Skulls, dancing skeletons, and blow kisses at the ceiling,
Whistling Great War numbers – 'Over There', 'It's a Long,
Long Way', 'Keep the Home Fires Burning' (the refrain) –
As though for my father who could also whistle them,
Trench memories, your eyes closed, your head tilted back,
Your cheeks filling up with air and melody and laughter.
I hold the banister. I touch your arm. Listen, Lucy,
There are songbirds circling high up in the stairwell.

AMELIA'S POEM

Amelia, your newborn name
Combines with the midwife's word
And, like smoke from driftwood fires,
Wafts over the lochside road
Past the wattle byre – hay bales
For ponies, Silver and Whisper –
Between drystone walls' river-
Rounded moss-clad ferny stones,
Through the fenceless gate and gorse
To the flat erratic boulder
Where otters and your mother rest,
Spraints black as your *meconium*,
Fish bones, fish scales, shitty sequins
Reflecting what light remains.

MARIGOLDS, 1960

You are dying. Why do we fight?
You find my first published poem –
'Not worth the paper it's printed on,'
You say. *She gave him marigolds –*

You are dying. 'They've cut out my
Wheesht – I have to sit down
To *wheesht* – like a woman' –
Marigolds *the colour of autumn –*

I need to hitchhike to Dublin
For Trinity Term. 'I'll take you
Part of the way,' you say,
'And we can talk if you like.'

And we talk and talk as though
We know we are just in time.
'A little bit further,' you say
Again and again, and in pain.

A few miles from Drogheda
You turn the car. We say goodbye
And you drive away slowly
Towards Belfast and your death.

To keep in his cold room. Look
At me now on the Newry Road
Standing beside my rucksack. Och,
Daddy, look in your driving mirror.

BOAT
for Seamus

What's the Greek for boat,
You ask, old friend,
Fellow voyager
Approaching Ithaca –
Oh, flatulent sails,
Wave-winnowing oars,
Shingle-scrunching keel –
But, so close to home,
There's a danger always
Of amnesiac storms,
Waterlogged words.

THE BROIGHTER BOAT
for Marie

A friend wears as a brooch
Gold boat, golden oars,
Refinement intensified
Below her breastbone,

Mast, oars, tiller
Hammered thin as ash
Keys, sycamore wings,
Rowlocks whispering,

Her journey's replica
With me a stowaway,
A transubstantial
Imaginary oarsman.

LIZARD ORCHID

I

All ears in the Mugello
What with the far cuckoo,
The harmonising frog
And crickets everywhere,
Domestic sounds as well –
Heidi baking a chestnut
Cake, Lorenzo's ladder
Scraping the cherry tree –
We find in Silvano's
Sloping upper meadow
Close to the wood, regal
Among seeding grasses,
An orchid, each lower lip
A streamer, extroversion
Requiring subtle breezes,
A name to silence cuckoo
And frog, lizard orchid.

II

Did the muddy boots of Tommies
Really bring back to England
From the Great War lizard-orchid
Seeds – stalks taller than you'd think,
Tongues little-finger-long, ribbons
For widow hats – dead soldiers
Returning, adhesive souls?

BOY-SOLDIER

The spear-point pierces his tender neck.
His armour clatters as he hits the ground.
Blood soaks his hair, bonny as the Graces',
Braids held in place by gold and silver bands.
Think of a smallholder who rears a sapling
In a beauty spot a burn burbles through
(You can hear its music close to your home)
Milky blossoms quivering in the breeze.
A spring blizzard blows in from nowhere
And uproots it, laying its branches out.
Thus Euphorbus, the son of Pantheus,
A boy-soldier – the London Scottish, say,
The Inniskillings, the Duke of Wellington's –
Was killed and despoiled by Menelaus.

from FOR PETER, MY TWIN

The Trees

I dreamed we were cutting down the trees
Of childhood: at the back of our garden
The grey ash from which we dropped into
The playing fields, two flowering currants'
Summer hum, the cherry tree that after
Many barren years produced five pears,
The sickly apple tree, the beautiful
Poisonous laburnum, and the cypress
That was impossible to climb. Peter,
If you hide in there, I'll never find you.

The Feet
for Catherine

You showed me my twin's feet when he was dead,
Your sailor-husband's feet, your engineer's – how
Cold they felt, how handsome ankle and toe,
Bone-shapes out of our gloomy womb-tangle –
A god's immortal feet, I'll dare to think,
When we scatter his ashes in the North Sea
Off the windy pier at Whitburn Village –
Poseidon, say, who drives his chariot's bronze-
Hoofed horses so headlong over the waves
All the sea-creatures know who it must be
And the sea parts with a kind of happiness
And the axle doesn't even get wet.

The Apparition

'Are you asleep, Achilles? Have you forgotten me?
Bury me quickly, please, and let me through Death's
Gates: exhausted ghosts get in the way and keep me
From crossing the River to join them: a lost soul
I sleepwalk on the wrong side of the gateway.
Let me hold your hand: once you've cremated me
I'll never come back again out of the darkness.
Never again will you and I sit down together
To make plans, a discreet distance from our friends.
My birthright, Death's abominable night-terror,
Overwhelms me now: your destiny too is fixed,
God-like Achilles: death below the Trojan walls.
One more request: bury our bones together
In the gold two-handled jar your mother gave you.'

'Patroclus, dear brother, I shall do as you ask:
I'll see to the arrangements for your funeral. But
Come closer now, for a moment let us embrace
And wail in excruciating lamentation.'
He reached out but he couldn't get hold of him:
Like smoke the hallucination slipped away
Bat-squeaking underground. Achilles, flabbergasted,
Threw up his hands and blurted out heartbroken words:
'Even in the House of Death something remains,
A ghost or image, but there's no real life in it.
All night the apparition of sad Patroclus
Has hovered over me, weeping and keening
And giving instructions. Did I imagine him?
He looked so like himself, a double, a twin.'

The Bay

You'd have loved the funeral games, Peter
– Sports-crazy, our Patroclus, a true Greek –
The chariot race, squabbles about the spoils,
One horse in particular, out in front,
A bay, reddish brown all over except for
The blaze on his forehead, round as the moon.

The Boxers

We were combatants from the start. Our dad
Bought us boxing gloves when we were ten –
Champions like Euryalus, say, or Epeius
Of wooden-horse fame: 'I am the greatest!'
'Nobody's going to knock me down!' Listen,
Peter, to the commentary – gruesome teeth-
Grinding, sweat splattering their arms and legs,
Huge fists in ox-hide thongs slugging it out,
Then the knock-out blow to Euryalus's chin –
Hoisting him with an uppercut – like a fish
That arches out of weed-tangled shallows
And collapses back into hazy water,
Sea wind sending shock-waves up the beach –
The winner gives the loser a helping hand
And his seconds support him across the ring
On dragging feet, head lolling to one side,
Blood clots et cetera et cetera . . .
I'll tie your gloves. Shall we fight again?

The Birthday

This is our first birthday without you,
My twin, July the twenty-seventh.
Where are you now? I'm looking out for you.
Have you been skinny-dipping at Allaran
Where the jellies won't sting, or in the lake
Among the reeds and damsel flies, sandwort
Stars at your feet, grass of parnassus in bud?
This year the residential swans have cygnets,
Four of them. They won't mind you splashing,
Nor will the sandpipers eyeing Dooaghtry
For a nesting place among the pebbles
At the samphire line. Now you know the spot.
Choughs flock high above their acrobatic
Cliff face and call to you antiquated
Expletives *pshaw pshaw pshaw*. Again and
Again I mention the erratic boulder
Because so much happens there, five hares
In the morning, then a squiggle of stoats.
I've boiled organic beetroots for supper.
Will your pee be pink in heaven? Oh,
The infinite gradations of sunset here.
Thank you for visiting Carrigskeewaun.
Don't twist your ankle in a rabbit hole.
I'll carry the torch across the duach.

The Duckboards

The longer way round from Carrigskeewaun
Goes past the bottom of the second lake,
Through salt marsh and yellow flags, and over
Rotten duckboards I wouldn't venture on
Except to look for rare helleborines,
The mallard's nest in its grassy well, or
Our father's ghost, as though at Passchendaele,
Teetering on walkways that disappear
As we follow behind him in the rain.

The Twins

Our representatives in the chariot race
Would have to be the twin Moliones,
Kteatos and Eurytos, Aktor's sons
(Though their real father was Poseidon) –
Siamese twins, joined below the waist,
One grasping the reins for dear life,
The other whipping the horses to win,
Two souls, one well-balanced charioteer
Taking the trophy and this epitaph.

The Fire

I press the button at your funeral.
The curtains close behind your coffin.
Can you hear the wind in high branches
Howling at its angriest, a bellows
That kindles sparks in hillside clearings
And incinerates the whole woodland?

PINE MARTENS

Amelia is making up her own tunes
By first light, a shrew and field-mouse
Aubade, a cradle-song for nestlings
That escape the green woodpecker,
Her improvisations a mist-net
That entangles John Campbell's ghost
Who lived here years ago and fed
The pine martens and walked depressed
Down the burnside boreen in his socks
To Lochalsh and drowned himself there,
Her notes lamentation and welcome
For punctual pine martens scratching
The kitchen window for bread and jam.

SOLSTICE

Hoping for otter-encounters
I walk without grandchildren
Into the Lochalsh silence,
The puddle-lit salt-marsh,
But curlews give me away
And I concentrate instead
On the low sun as it frays
Through a tree-creeper's useful
Fan-tail (unlike the nuthatch
It can climb only upwards
In spirals, bark-mouse, crevice-
Snoozer), before I turn to face
My elongated shadow
With its walking stick, and
The cottage where grandchildren
Draw in closer to the stove
On the shortest day, above them
Bracken-rusty Angel Hill.

NATIVITY

A starring role without any words,
The Virgin Mary wearing specs,
Maisie, little flat-chested mother
In your blue brushed-cotton robe,

The antique spongeware bowl you hold
With its abstract leafy pattern
(A Scottish fir tree) is for washing
The imaginary baby in.

In the darkness after the play
You watch December's meteors
(The Geminids) over Angel Hill
Coincide with the northern lights,

And carry home the spongeware bowl
Very carefully, still unbroken
After birth-pangs and stage-fright and
Large enough to hold the whole world.

FIFTY YEARS

You have walked with me again and again
Up the stony path to Carrigskeewaun
And paused among the fairy rings to pick
Mushrooms for breakfast and for poetry.

You have pointed out, like a snail's shell
Or a curlew feather or mermaid's purse,
The right word, silences and syllables
Audible at the water's windy edge.

We have tracked otter prints to Allaran
And waited for hours on our chilly throne,
For fifty years, man and wife, voices low,
Counting oystercatchers and sanderlings.

SNOWDROPS

Inauspicious between headstones
On Angel Hill, wintry love-
Tokens for Murdo, Alistair,
Duncan, home from the trenches,
Back in Balmacara and Kyle,
Cameronians, Gordon Highlanders
Clambering on hands and knees
Up the steep path to this graveyard
The snowdrops whiten, green-
Hemmed frost-piercers, buttonhole
Or posy, Candlemas bells
For soldiers who come here on leave
And rest against rusty railings
Like out-of-breath pallbearers.

THE SONNETS
for Vanessa Davis

The soldier-poet packed into his kitbag
His spine-protector, socks, soap, latherbrush
(Though he was not then a regular shaver)
Water-bottle, field-dressing, gas-mask, a tin
Of cigarettes (a gift from Princess Mary,
The girl next door at Buckingham Palace),
Housewife, bootlaces, pull-through, paybook
And the sonnets of William Shakespeare.

He brushed off the mud at Passchendaele and,
Before going over the top, tucked away
In his breastpocket the leatherbound book
Which stopped a bullet just short of his heart
And shredded the life-saving poetry. He
Inhaled one of Princess Mary's Woodbines.

THE POETS
poem beginning with a line of John Clare

Poets love nature and themselves are love.
Imagine an out-of-the-way cottage
Close to dunes, the marram grass whispering
Above technicolour snails and terns' eggs,
Intelligent choughs on the roof at dawn,
At dusk whimbrels whistling down the chimney,
And outside the kitchen window that cliff
Where ravens have nested for fifty years.

Moth-and-butterfly-wing decipherers,
Counters of Connemara ponies and swans,
Along the lazybeds at the lake's edge
They materialise out of sea-mist and
Into hawkbit haziness disappear.
One has written a lovely blackbird poem.

THE TROUBLES

Think of the children
Behind the coffins.
Look sorrow in the face.
Call those thirty years
The Years of Disgrace.

AGE

I have been writing about this townland
For fifty years, watching on their hummock
Autumn lady's tresses come and go and,
After a decade underground, return
In hundreds. I have counted the whoopers
And the jackdaws over Morrison's barn.
Too close on the duach to tractor tracks
The ringed plover's nest has kept me awake,
And the otter that drowned in an eel-trap.
Salvaging snail shells and magpie feathers
For fear of leaving particulars out,
I make little space for philosophising.
I walk ever more slowly to gate and stile.
Poetry is shrinking almost to its bones.

MATISSE

Wielding a colossal pair of scissors,
Cutting out from the costliest paper
The world's peculiar shapes, he instructed
From his wheelchair beautiful assistants
Where to position – floor to ceiling –
Each adhesive genesis, cloud formations
Reflected in estuarial waters.

He covered a stain on his studio wall
With a swallow's cut-out shape, then added
Other birds and fish and coral and leaves,
Memory replacing the outside world
And his imagination a lagoon
Where, immobile, he swam every day
Contemplating his submarine kingdom.

ORPEN

Orpen in the trenches
Sketching skeletons –
Breast bone, ankle bone,
Vertebrae, pelvis –
Sets up his easel
On the bomb crater's rim
And paints the armistice.

ORS

I

I am standing on the canal bank at Ors
Willing Wilfred Owen to make it across
To the other side where his parents wait.
He and his men are constructing pontoons.
The German sniper doesn't know his poetry.

II

My daughter Rebecca lives in twenty-four
Saint Bernard's Crescent opposite the home
Wilfred visited for 'perfect little dinners'
And 'extraordinary fellowship in all the arts'.
I can hear him on his way to the Steinthals.

III

Last year I read my own poems at Craiglockhart
And eavesdropped on Robert, Siegfried, Wilfred
Whispering about poetry down the corridors.
If Wilfred can concentrate a little longer,
He might just make it to the other bank.

MOTHS & BUTTERFLIES

I want to talk to dead children
About moths and butterflies,
The Peacock's eyespots, two
Then four, beauty and terror;
Six Spot Burnet's warning
Black and red (hydrogen
Cyanide); the female
Winter moth that cannot fly;
And one with no proboscis
That cannot feed, a ghetto moth;
Caterpillars that gobble
Stinging nettles and ragwort;
Nightmares of the chrysalis.

In September forty-four
Hanuš Hachenburg writes
Somewhere, far away out there,
Childhood sweetly sleeps
Along that path among the trees;
Listen to Pavel Friedmann
I never saw another
Butterfly, that butterfly
Was the last one, butterflies
Don't live in the ghetto;
I want to talk to dead children,
The children of Terezín,
About moths and butterflies.

DANDELIONS

The children can still be heard,
Their memories growing fainter
And fainter. Listen. Listen.
Just look up to heaven
And think about the violets
One whispers, and another
The dandelions call to me
And the white chestnut branches.

PRIMO'S QUESTION

How can you murder millions of people
In the middle of Europe and not know?
Look out the window at those miserable lines,
Prisoners fainting and dying of exhaustion
In the long streets and at railway stations.
How can you murder millions and not know?

SEDGE-WARBLERS

Callimachus joins me at your grave
Who shed tears for Heraclitus
And said his poems were nightingales
That death would never lay hands on.
There are no nightingales in Ireland
But sedge-warblers sometimes sing at night
And are mistaken for nightingales,
So death that snatches at everything
Will leave untouched in Bellaghy
Your poems, the sedge-warbler's song.

POEM

I am the candlelight master
Striking a match in the shadows.
A smoky wick, then radiance.
I am the candlelight master.

AFTER AMERGIN

I am the trout that vanishes
Between the stepping stones.
I am the elver that lingers
Under the little bridge.
I am the leveret that breakfasts
Close to the fuchsia hedge.
I am the stoat that dances
Around the erratic boulder.
I am the skein of sheep's wool
Wind and barbed wire tangle.
I am the mud and spittle
That make the swallows' nest.
I am the stonechat's music
Of pebble striking pebble.
I am the overhead raven
With his eye on the lamb's eye.
I am the night-flying whimbrel
That whistles down the chimney.
I am the pipistrelle bat
At home among constellations.
I am the raindrop enclosing
Fairy flax or brookweed.
I am waterlily blossom
And autumn lady's tresses.
I am the thunderstorm
That penetrates the keyhole.
I am the sooty hailstone
Melting by the fireside.
I am the otter's holt and
The badger's sett in the dunes.
I am the badger drowning
At spring tide among flotsam.
I am the otter dying
On top of the burial mound.

TO OTOMO YAKAMOCHI
on receiving the inaugural Yakamochi Medal

You, Otomo Yakamochi,
Poet and governor, and I
Minor bureaucrat, and poet too,
Meet across thirteen hundred years
To talk about birds and flowers.

Lover of cuckoos and wisteria,
For you I have saved meadowsweet
And willowherb and loosestrife
And the meadow pipit's few notes
And the skylark's aria.

We gaze on our soul-landscapes
More intensely with every year –
Small boats passing Inishbofin,
Small boats on the Nago Sea,
Wokami River crimson-lustrous.

Barnacle geese our messengers
Across space and time, Otomo –
Tormentil closed by the rain
And centaury, tiny boxes
Yellow and pink, Japanese.

Anything however small
May make a poem, a snail, say,
Tucked into the marram grass,
In the distance Tateyama
Or Mweelrea, holy mountains.

I picture you at the White Strand
Galloping through the breakers,
Spring-tide and rain and spray
Kicked up by your horse's hooves
Drenching bridle and stirrups.

A small townland becomes my life,
Carrigskeewaun, grandchildren
Wading in the tidal channel –
Otomo, my soul's a currach
Disappearing behind the waves.

GRASS OF PARNASSUS

High up on Tateyama
(Of Japan's holy mountains
Yakamochi's favourite)
We find by a stony path
A solitary overlooked
Grass of parnassus in flower
And stoop to decipher
Engraved petals, and to share
Across the millennium
With the flower-loving poet
The white gleam we first noticed
Amid eyebright and speedwell
At far-off Carrigskeewaun
Years ago, and still in bud.

WAR

I

Because he was his youngest
And dearest child, old Priam
Begged Polydorus not to fight,
But this champion athlete
Wanted to show off his speed
And in a foolhardy display
Raced against the front-runners –
Until he died, for Achilles
Was just as fast and struck him
With his javelin full in the back
Where the golden belt-buckles
Fastened his leather corselet,
The spear-point penetrating
Right through to his navel
And he fell to his knees groaning
And blacking out and clasping
In his hands his intestines.

II

When Hector saw his brother
Polydorus on the ground
Mortally wounded, blacking out,
His intestines in his hands –
His eyes misted over with tears
And he made straight for Achilles
Flaunting his javelin like a flame.

EMPTY CHARIOTS

Many horses with high-arching necks
Made their empty chariots clatter along
Down the lines of battle, in mourning
For their irreplaceable charioteers
Who lay on the battlefield, far dearer
To the vultures than to their wives.

MOLY

Translating the *Iliad* at Corragaun –
Book Twenty – Achilles' rampage –
I turn to the *Odyssey* for relief
And stroll from my sheepskin armchair
Down the overgrown pebbly path
To search among goose-grass and centaury
And scarlet pimpernel for that milk-
White flower with black root, so difficult
For mortal man to find, occult herb
And antidote for spells – Circe's spells –
Nobody knows exactly what it is
But I shall recognise it if it's here
(Its name among the gods is Moly)
And Inishturk becomes Ithaca.

WILD ORCHIDS

In my synapses early purples persevering
As in a muddy tractor track across the duach;
Close to the old well and the skylarks' nest, briefly
Marsh helleborines surviving the cattle's hooves,
Then re-emerging at the waterlily lake
Between the drystone wall and otter corridors;
A stone's throw from the Carrigskeewaun cottage
Two introverted frog orchids; in the distance
A hummock covered with autumn lady's tresses,
Ivory spirals that vanish for a decade;
On the higher bank of the Owenadornaun
Above the sandmartins' nesting holes, butterfly
Orchids like ballerinas; at Kilnaboy
Bee orchids under the sheela-na-gig's display;
Dowdy *neotinea maculata* at my feet
Where the turlough below Mullaghmore disappears
Underground; against limestone grey at Black Head
Red helleborines igniting; the lesser twayblade
With its flower spike like a darning needle, tiny
And hidden away beneath a heather stand;
On the Tyrrells' Kildalkey farm, pink pyramids;
Along the path to the waterfall at Cardoso,
Near Elvira's overgrown olive grove, tongue
Orchids folded like napkins; lizard orchids
In the Mugello, shaggy, thigh-high; on Paros
Bee orchids (again) beside the marble pavement,
A blackcap singing (in Greece or Ireland?); just one
Bedraggled fly orchid in a forgotten field,
Its petals cobalt, chestnut-brown, as I recall.

SONNET FOR MICHAEL VINEY

I have walked with him along the yellow strand
Beachcombing for words among hieroglyphics,
And up the hill to a big tarn, around Mweelrea
To Derry, the deserted village, through fences
To oak woods draped with lichens at Old Head
Or Brackloon below Croagh Patrick, and watched
The sun rolling down the Reek, a ball of fire.

He has shown me beetle tracks in the sand dunes,
Microscopic snails, one nearly invisible
Flower called petalwort, a peregrine falcon
And the cloud beyond with its inky rim,
Dead-nettle and chickweed, a stream's tattle.
From his 'thorn-edged acre' at Thallabaun
We gaze into the depths of the Milky Way.

THE WALK
for Jeffrey Morgan

If you hadn't come all the way with me
Along Thallabaun strand when I pointed out
Bottlenose dolphins surfacing between
The islands and suggested they might foretell
An otter if we could brave the sandy wind
And wait for an hour at Allaran Point,
And after only minutes a bitch otter
Paused on rocks just feet away, sea water
Streaming from her whiskers, our thumping hearts
Audible surely, and as we stood to stretch
A family of whooper swans, two white
And three grey, circled above our heads
On their way from Iceland to Carrigskeewaun,
No one would believe these three visitations,
And you quipped what's next then, and yes, old friend,
What's next, what's next, what's next, what's next?

BROTHER

That Catullus line – *multas per gentes* –
Applies to you, my marine engineer
Circumnavigating the globe, and me
Following you in my imagination
Across many a sea to speak in vain
To your ashes. My twin torn from my life,
Accept this elegy wet with my weeping.
Steer your tanker towards eternity –
Greetings, dear sailor, my brother, goodbye.

DECEMBER

I shall be eighty soon.
I go on looking for
The Geminids somewhere
Between Cassiopeia
And the big beech tree.

TAWNY OWL

At least the motorist who stunned the owl
Stopped and lifted the body onto the verge
And there Amelia and Maisie found it.
A friend will soak the wings in salty water
To make shaman-fans for smudging rites,
Another wants the skull for her collection
And will have to bury it for one whole year.
(Why are there no tawny owls in Ireland?
Do you know that Eric Hosking photograph
Of the tawny that robbed him of an eye,
Rage and terror cramped between the branches?)
Maisie sketches in charcoal its underside,
Amelia hugs to herself all the feathers:
'I will look after you, poor owl,' she sighs.

EYELID

Amelia opens the tawny owl's eyelid
And finds a concentration of the night.

AMELIA'S MODEL

I

In her model of the solar system
My seven-year-old cosmologist
Ties to a barbeque skewer
With fuse wire the planets, buttons:
For Venus an ivory button,
Mercury silver beside the sun,
Mother-of-pearl for Jupiter,
Red and green for Mars and Earth,
For Saturn's rings a pipe-cleaner,
So that in the outer darkness
Close to the kitchen her brown eyes
Represent Uranus, Neptune.

II

Amelia, you didn't include Pluto
In your wire sculpture of the solar system:
Tiny and very far away, an ice
World of ice mountains and methane snow,
A dance of five moons unlit by the sun,
The god of the afterlife's kingdom –
We shall go there when we die, dear child.

QUATRAINS

I

What did they talk about on picnic trips,
The concentration camp's senior staff?
To whom did they post their happy photos,
'Lots of love from all of us at Auschwitz'?

II

They put up a Christmas tree in Auschwitz
And stacked as presents underneath the tree
Bodies of prisoners who had died that day.
Then the assembled ranks sang 'Silent Night'.

III

The deadly smoke belching night and day
And screams from the tortured and dying
Meant that birds stopped singing at Auschwitz.
Sanity was remembering their names.

RAVINE

I

In a quiet Polish ravine
Two German soldiers with rifles
Can murder so many women.
Oh, their ageing breasts look sore.
Keep your blouses on, my dear ones.

II

Bullets are saved for slaughtering grown-ups
And are not wasted on little children
Who suffocate underneath their families
And drown in their parents' blood and urine.

LULLABY

When a ghetto baby dies
the mother sings a lullaby
lullay my child lullay lullay
her breasts are weeping milk
lullay my child lullay lullay

SOLOMON'S-SEAL

Shaded by the self-seeded hazels
In a back corner of our garden,
To the right of the flowering currant
An unexpected Solomon's-seal
I want to show you. Does it matter
Why such graceful bells are so called
(Seals of a medieval document?)
It's May, and Solomon says: *Rise up,*
My love, my fair one, and come away,
Winter is past, the rain is over
And gone, flowers appear on the earth.
A solitary cowslip has survived
Under our beech the first grass-cutting.
The time of the singing of birds is come.

SNEEZEWORT

Now that the virus keeps us apart
I try to remember exactly where
I introduced my first grandson
Years ago to this unassuming
Supposed cure for cough and cold,
And he drew a picture of it
Above spindly letters, sneezewort,
Petals arranged like a daisy's
Around a grey-and-yellow eye
That might irradiate sickness:
Was it where a runnel murmurs
Into the lake without a name?

CASSANDRA

Which songbird would I choose to represent
Cassandra – our own blackbird, or the nightingale
That gale-force winds have buffeted to Ireland
Or, lost in its vast aria, the wren, or the chiffchaff,
Or the redbreast foretelling the end of the world
In its autumn lament? Who will believe her song
When she faces the cameras and microphones?
The dawn chorus is broadcasting fake news.

TELEMACHOS

Daniel my son, my Telemachos,
Funnier than I am, far cleverer,
Crossword virtuoso, scrabble champ,
Professor of molecular biology
Waging war in your laboratory against
The ghastly crab, and with chemicals
Hoodwinking tumours to devour themselves
(Would Hermes' gift of moly be any use,
That antidote for Circe's sorcery –
Only an onion some scholars think – so
How about poetry's abracadabra
Which gives everything a second chance?)
You wait for my return to Ithaca,
You keep me going on this odyssey.

TAKABUTI

in the Ulster Museum

My granddaughters stare down at her,
A petite fashion-conscious Egyptian
Not much older than they are, her face
Darkened by incense and time, her linen
Eyeballs returning their gaze, her hand
By her side as though to welcome them,
Her foot poking out of the bandages
As though to follow them to the exit
And accompany the rest of their lives.

ORIGAMI

Why shouldn't they make use of my failures,
Early versions, outlines, my granddaughters
Conjuring frogs and birds out of scrap paper
And laying my lost words on a swan's wing?

AMATEUR

In his last years my dad took up painting,
Imagined landscapes to begin with – yachts
That snuggled in their harbour, overwhelmed
By a huge geranium in the foreground –
'I want to grab hold of the stem,' I said.
We hung it cheaply framed above the piano.
Then, a re-arranged Donegal – haystacks
Where they were needed, a red wheelbarrow,
A yellowish towpath going nowhere.
Prognathous, chain-smoking, an amateur
Leaning into perpetual summertime,
Squeezing rainbows onto a dinner plate,
My dad painted to please himself and me,
For eternity a weekend painter –
'Should I move Muckish a little to the left?'

WRECK

Neighbours have pulled asunder my ship of death
– The old wreck with its cargo of sandy water –
Tractors and ropes and chains on Thallabaun strand,
Spars hard as stone dismembered for gate-posts
And barn-lintels. Where are the tree-pegs now
That held together my oblivion-boat
At the edge of the surf among sanderlings?
At spring tide where will my soul be going?

TOTEM

When the tree-surgeon cut away
From our top-heavy beech a ton,
I assembled in my mind's eye logs
As a star-surrounded totem pole
With carvings of all the creatures –
Concussed tawny owl, sleepy
Pot-bellied badger, otter drowned
In the eel-trap, Rosemary's donkeys,
Emma's punctual frogs, hares
And stoats playing scary games
Around the erratic boulder – O all
In a ghost dance with my twin brother
And the dead poets and my warrior
Father and my mother with her limp.

INDEX OF TITLES